I0811781

REMARKABLE

WOMEN

of the

OUTER BANKS

REMARKABLE WOMEN of the OUTER BANKS

Hannah Bunn West

THE History PRESS

Published by The History Press
Charleston, SC
www.historypress.com

Copyright © 2022 by Hannah Bunn West
All rights reserved

First published 2022

Manufactured in the United States

ISBN 9781467146029

Library of Congress Control Number: 2021952410

Notice: The information in this book is true and complete to the best of our knowledge. It is offered without guarantee on the part of the author or The History Press. The author and The History Press disclaim all liability in connection with the use of this book.

All rights reserved. No part of this book may be reproduced or transmitted in any form whatsoever without prior written permission from the publisher except in the case of brief quotations embodied in critical articles and reviews.

For Hazel, my girl

CONTENTS

ACKNOWLEDGMENTS

I am humbled by the help and support I received from the Outer Banks community in writing this book. I want to sincerely thank everyone who sat down to speak with me, answered my questions, helped locate resources or lent their support. Special thanks go to Tama Creef and Stuart Parks II at the Outer Banks History Center for helping me to source the majority of the images for this book. Dorothy Hope, Chaz Winkler, Janis Raye Raphel, Tammi Raye Pittaro, Marlysa Raye Jacobus, Ann-Cabell Baum, Cheryl Shelton-Roberts and Marilyn Berry Morrison shared with me the stories of their loved ones' lives. Ladd Bayliss with the Outer Banks Conservationists, Jami Lanier with the National Park Service, Kate Jenkins and Zoe Ames with The History Press and all of the incredible staff who aided me at the libraries, archives, museums and universities that I utilized were invaluable. These institutions not only preserve our collective human history but also inform our path forward. Thank you to UNCW's Creative Writing Department and all of my professors, classmates and fond memories there, and to Lauren Cowart for her photography. I'm grateful to my family, my friends and everyone who believed in this project and helped me to complete it, especially my husband, Aaron West, and our children, Hazel and Isaac. Lastly, thank you to the Outer Banks and its people. There's no place I would have rather grown up.

INTRODUCTION

Outer Bankers have long been known for their resourcefulness and grit. They are daring, resilient, inventive and sometimes stubborn. The Outer Banks is represented by a faint line on most maps—if at all—yet steeped in history and legend. It is composed of a strand of barrier islands running parallel to North Carolina's mainland from the Virginia border south to Ocracoke Inlet. Known for sandy, windswept beaches that meet the Atlantic on their eastern edge, with a network of maritime forests, marshes and sounds to the west, the area is relatively isolated and unique environmentally and culturally. Anyone who has spent time on the Outer Banks can tell you that it operates by a set of rules that don't always apply to the rest of the world. Its local history boasts seafaring explorers, notorious pirates, stoic lifesavers and the world's first airplane pilots. Yet some of the area's notable tales and accomplishments are lesser known. In this book, you'll meet women throughout the course of the Outer Banks' colorful history and hear their stories of courage, risk-taking and adventure on these sandy stretches at the edge of the world.

For several years, I worked at the historic First Colony Inn in Nags Head, and each day that I reported for my shift felt like a step back in time. Brass keys hung from hooks behind the front desk, one for each room. Ledger books from the 1940s were kept in the second-floor library; their tattered, handwritten pages recorded the guests who checked in and the bottles of milk and other provisions purchased each day. I felt safe in the old building, enveloped by its cedar shingles and wraparound porches. The guest rooms, dining area, kitchen and library emanated a warmth that came from decades of collective human activity. An imprint of enchantment lingered in the space. I used to picture the building as if a cross section had been taken from it, like looking at a dollhouse where you can see into all the rooms at once. If not for a woman named Camille Lawrence, the 1930s-era hotel would have been demolished in 1988 by a developer who wanted to put duplexes on the oceanfront acreage. He planned to burn the hotel to the ground. After the Nags Head Board of Commissioners prohibited the burning of historic buildings in response, the developer offered to sell the inn for one dollar to anyone who would move it off of the property. Camille and her husband, Richard, purchased the storm-damaged structure and relocated it to family-owned land between the highways at the 15.5 milepost, where it is still open and welcoming guests to this day.

As I drove home from the inn each night, I would pass by other pieces of Outer Banks history and think about the women we had to thank for their preservation. The hulking mass of Jockey's Ridge silhouetted in moonlight would have been flattened if Carolista Baum had not taken a stand. The shelves in Mattie Midgett's old general store held decades of beachcombed objects collected by her daughter, Nellie Myrtle, a chronicle of our material history. To the south, the Cape Hatteras Lighthouse stood tall but could have been a pile of black-and-white bricks in the ocean if not for the advocacy of Cheryl Shelton-Roberts.

In conducting research for this book, it was often difficult to find substantial historical records pertaining to women. It would seem that the names, dates and details linked to their lives weren't always viewed as consequential enough to be recorded. Their letters and journals were not the ones being saved or published. For example, we have detailed sixteenth-century accounts of the Roanoke Island expeditions by John White, Thomas Hariot and Ralph Lane, yet no written account by Eleanor Dare or other women in the colony. The lack of records was especially apparent when researching people of color. For example, enslaved persons were listed in census records by race and gender only, assigned a number instead of a name. They were classed as a commodity. There was fluidity in the surnames of formerly enslaved people, in that many assumed the last name of the slaveholder family that claimed ownership of them, then later inherited or chose to go by a different name after emancipation. As for the Algonquian people that were the area's original inhabitants prior to European contact, detailed accounts from the colonial era are scant. Any existing historical records, outside of physical artifacts that have been uncovered, were written by European men and presented within the context of their outsiders' understanding. The watercolors of John White, who was commissioned as an artist on the 1585 expedition to Roanoke and then named governor of the ill-fated 1587 colony, provide a valuable visual record of the people of the Carolina coast almost five hundred years ago. However, many of his portraits depict their subjects in poses that were popular in Elizabethan artwork of the time. As a result, we see the Indigenous people of the Outer Banks through a European lens. People with Algonquian ancestry still call the Outer Banks home today, though they were often overlooked, misrepresented and/or unrecognized by official records in decades past and even into the present day.

Though some of their stories were hard to uncover and though their backgrounds are diverse, each of these women swam against the tide in her day and age. It is said that well-behaved women seldom make history. This depends, however, on how you define misbehavior. If it means charting your own course, taking a stand or speaking out to effect change, the women in these pages misbehaved indeed. The aim of this book, then, is to highlight them in our remarkable history.

Chapter 1

A NEW LIFE

Eleanor Dare, 1580s

Eleanor Dare was well into her third trimester when she arrived on the shores of Roanoke Island in 1587. She, along with over one hundred men, women and children, had set sail from England and endured a three-month ocean passage to reach the "New World." They came ashore in July, a month that marks the height of summer in coastal North Carolina. Temperatures reach into the nineties; mosquitoes swarm, and high humidity overwhelms. In addition to the exhausting and disorienting effects of travel, Eleanor would have been experiencing intensifying physical symptoms as her body prepared for childbirth—swelling, fatigue, shortness of breath, insomnia and body aches, to name a potential few. While she is memorialized throughout history as the mother of the first English child born in the New World, we don't often consider the peril she was thrown into on these shores or the tragedy that befell the native inhabitants.

A Time Before "the Outer Banks": Mapping the Carolina Sounds in the Sixteenth Century

In the sixteenth century, the area we now call the Outer Banks was a part of what the English called Virginia, named for their virgin queen, Elizabeth I. It had been "discovered" by the English in 1584 when Philip Amadas and Arthur Barlowe voyaged on behalf of Sir Walter Raleigh to explore a potential site for an English colony overseas. To the land's

Jill Voight played the role of Eleanor Dare during *The Lost Colony's* 1969 season. Here she depicts the young mother on the shores of a strange land. *Photo courtesy of the Outer Banks History Center, Aycock Brown Papers.*

Indigenous inhabitants, the area was known as Ossomocomuck. They were Algonquian-speaking people who naturally "did not consider the place they lived a new world," as author Michael Leroy Oberg explains in his book *The Head in Edward Nugent's Hand: Roanoke's Forgotten Indians*. His researched narrative centers the Algonquian people in the story of Roanoke Island, shifting the perspective from the English explorers who, despite claiming and naming the land for their queen, "intruded into an environment where Indian rules prevailed."[1]

Ossomocomuck stretched from the border of modern-day Virginia south to Bogue Inlet and included the barrier islands of the present-day Outer Banks to the east and a swath of the coastal North Carolina mainland to the west. The islands, like Roanoke, that lay in the sounds between these two points were included in the domain of Ossomocomuck as well.

Roanoke in particular was named for "the people who rub, abrade, smooth or polish by hand."[2] This likely referred to the shell beads that the island's

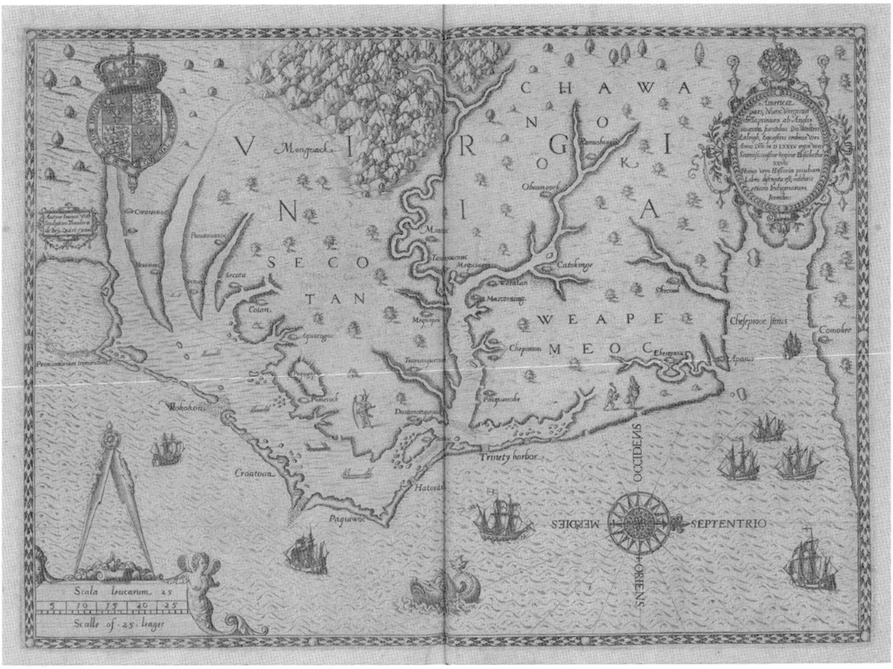

A sixteenth-century map of the coast from Chesapeake Bay to Cape Lookout, made by John White. It shows the locations of Algonquian villages, including "Roanoac." *Photo courtesy of the John Carter Brown Library.*

inhabitants were known to make and wear. Ossomocomuck was made up of dozens of independent communities, including Roanoke, Croatoan on Hatteras Island and Dasemunkepeuc in modern-day Manns Harbor. Though autonomous, the communities were interconnected and likely all under the authority of an Algonquian leader, or *weroance*, named Wingina.[3] Though it is not widely known or taught, we could point to his tragic end as a catalyst of the demise of the ill-fated 1587 colony on Roanoke Island.

THE 1587 COLONY WAS BOUND FOR THE CHESAPEAKE BAY

The Lost Colony, an acclaimed outdoor drama that tells the story of Sir Walter Raleigh's 1587 colony, has been captivating audiences on the Outer Banks since it was first performed in 1937. But the arrival of the colonists on

Roanoke Island was not marked by providence as much as this cherished story would lead us to believe. Eleanor Dare and the other men, women and children were effectively stranded on the island when the expedition's pilot, Simon Fernando, refused to take them any further.

John White, the father of Eleanor Dare, was an artist who had been on previous voyages to Roanoke Island and was appointed governor of the 1587 colony. His watercolors provide an unprecedented glimpse of life on America's Eastern Seaboard in the sixteenth century, and his journals provide us with a detailed (though one-sided) account of the expeditions to Roanoke Island. His account of the 1587 voyage is fraught with mistrust and disdain for the expedition's Portuguese pilot, Simon Fernando.

To imagine Eleanor's discomfort during the long journey is something that none of the existing accounts of the voyage attempt to do. But anyone who has carried a child or been in a close relationship with someone who has can intuit how miserable it likely was for her. On their way to Virginia, their ships stopped in Saint Croix on June 22, where they went ashore for several days. John White wrote in his journal that after eating some type of small green apple, some of the men and women were "fearfully troubled with a sudden burning in their mouths, and swelling of their tongues so big, that some of them could not speak." Eleanor may have watched in horror as "a child, by sucking one of those women's breasts, had at that instant his mouth set on such a burning that it was strange to see how the infant was tormented for the time." White also wrote of the colonists washing in a standing pool of water and that "their faces did so burn and swell that their eyes were shut up and could not see in five or six days longer."[4]

With their ships finally anchored off Hatteras, White wrote that on July 22, 1587, he and forty men prepared to sail a smaller ship, or pinnace, to Roanoke Island ahead of the other colonists. Their aim was to locate fifteen Englishmen from the 1585 expedition who had been left there by Sir Richard Grenville, "have conference concerning the state of the Country and savages," then "return again to the fleet and pass along the coast to the bay of Chesapeake."[5] It was then, as they sailed off from the larger ship, that Simon Fernando called to John White, ordering him "not to bring any of the [colonists] back again, but leave them in the Island," and declaring that "he would land all the [colonists] in no other place."[6]

Simon Fernando was refusing to take them any further. With summer nearing its end, he was anxious to return to Europe to encounter Spanish ships that he might privateer. At least, this was the excuse he gave. He had no apparent interest in the success of White's colony and effectively stranded the 117 men, women and children on Roanoke Island. It was only ever meant to be a stopover on the way to their final destination on the Chesapeake Bay, where they hoped to establish the first permanent English settlement on the North American continent. While Raleigh's 1584 and 1585 voyages to Roanoke had been largely military in nature, the vision for his 1587 colony was decidedly different. Chesapeake was chosen as the site for the "Cittie of Raleigh" for its location near a safe, deep-water anchorage where ships could easily reprovision and return to England. Rather than relying on the natives of the land for food, as the previous expeditions had, this colony would be a self-sufficient farming operation. Finally, to ensure the colony's permanence, women and children were needed. On board the ships were seventeen women and nine children that, along with the men, made up fourteen families. Two of the women, including Eleanor Dare, were pregnant, and from the account on Saint Croix we know of at least one other who was breastfeeding an infant.[7]

The caption by John White on this watercolor reads, "One of the wives of Wingina." The hairstyles, dress and ornamentation of the English women would have been very strange to the Algonquian women, and vice versa. *Photo courtesy of the Trustees of the British Museum.*

Sir Walter Raleigh envisioned his colonies in America as philanthropic endeavors that would bring civility, Christianity and other Anglo values to the "savages" that lived there (though competing with the French and Spanish for territory in the New World was certainly a motivator as well). This reveals the assumption of the English that the Algonquian-speaking people who inhabited the Outer Banks were uncivilized and in need of enlightenment or salvation. They, of course, did not view themselves this way. In an act of civility, they initially welcomed the English to the area and invited them to settle on Roanoke, interested in trade and allyship with the strange foreigners.

But what came to pass during Raleigh's attempted 1585 colony, which was the second expedition to Roanoke Island, deteriorated all hopes of peaceful cooperation and coexistence. In fact, it doomed the next group of outsiders who would set foot on the island, which happened to be the 117 men, women and children of the 1587 colony.

THE DEATH OF WINGINA AND ITS CONSEQUENCES FOR THE "LOST COLONY"

In the summer of 1586, one year before the "lost colonists" arrived on Roanoke Island, Ralph Lane had been left in charge of Raleigh's 1585 colony while Richard Grenville returned to England for supplies. There was tension between Lane and Wingina, who had recently changed his name to Pemisapan, and Lane suspected that he was conspiring to launch an attack on the colony. While some Roanoke and Croatoan leaders were friendly with the English, Wingina had decided to oppose them. He had initially extended his welcome, but as Lane and his men continued to put a burden on his people's food supply, took advantage of their generosity and began to demonstrate violence, relations started to degrade. Wingina, now Pemisapan, wished to cut ties with the English, but if anything, he hoped that they might starve and retreat.[8] Fearing an attack by Pemisapan's people, Lane decided to attack them first.

Wingina, who later changed his name to Pemisapan, depicted in a watercolor by John White. He was the leader, or weroance, of a network of Algonquian villages called Ossomocomuck. *Photo courtesy of the Trustees of the British Museum.*

Lane started by attacking the few Algonquians that remained on Roanoke Island. Most of them had relocated to Dasemunkepeuc across the sound (in modern-day Manns Harbor) shortly after Lane and his men built their fort on Roanoke Island. So that word of the attack would not reach Pemisapan in Dasemunkepeuc, Lane sent some of his men into the Croatan

Sound by night to intercept anyone who might be rowing back there from Roanoke. When the Englishmen encountered a canoe carrying two survivors, they overtook the Algonquians and cut off their heads. Word of Lane's attack never reached Pemisapan.

The next day on June 1, 1586, Pemisapan welcomed Ralph Lane and his men when they arrived at Dasemunkepeuc and waited for them to state their purpose. The English then opened fire, and Pemisapan was hit by a shot from a pistol. He fell to the ground, where the English assumed him dead. They continued to attack his people, as well as friendly Croatoans from Hatteras Island who often spent time at Dasemunkepeuc. Lane tried to avoid the Croatoans, but his men were indiscriminate in their assault.

Then, to Lane's surprise, Pemisapan "started up and ran away as though he had not been touched."[9] One of the soldiers fired a shot at the weroance that hit him in his rear, but he managed to escape into the woods. One of Lane's men, named Edward Nugent, chased after him and was gone a long time. Fearing that he had been overtaken or ambushed in the woods, the Englishmen went to search for Nugent. After a short while, they found him walking back out of the woods. He held in his hand the decapitated head of Pemisapan. Lane and his men returned to their fort on Roanoke, where they impaled the head of the weroance formerly known as Wingina on a pole.[10]

It was into the shadow of this vile attack that the 1587 colony came ashore one year later. Eleanor Dare was expecting her baby in a matter of weeks, a child that would be born in hostile territory due to the previous actions of her own countrymen. Lane's colony had doomed relations with the native people in the area for any Europeans that might come after them. Yet the story of Wingina's beheading and how it steered the course of the lost colonists' fate is often overlooked. Oberg writes:

> *Telling this story forces us to consider the question of just what constitutes a historically significant event, and who decides and why. The brutal act of violence executed by Edward Nugent is almost never specifically mentioned in history textbooks. His name, and that of the weroance he beheaded, are not commonly known. The crime, it seems, has been erased and silenced and forgotten, deemed not relevant to the larger narrative of American history. But the killing of this Algonquian leader had important consequences for the native peoples of the Carolina Sounds, and the short-lived English attempts at settlement brought misery and suffering that are difficult to imagine.*[11]

In the Wake of a Hurricane: Ralph Lane's Early Departure from Roanoke

After beheading the Algonquian leader, Lane and his men made a hasty retreat. Realizing the imminent danger of staying on Roanoke Island, they caught the first ship back to England. This ship belonged to Sir Francis Drake, who arrived off the Outer Banks one week after the murder of Wingina. After hearing what happened at Dasemunkepeuc, he offered Lane additional supplies and a small ship so that he could relocate his colony to Chesapeake if need be, but the weather decided their fate. A hurricane battered the island for four days, driving some of Drake's ships out to sea and sinking others. After the storm, Drake no longer had a ship fit to leave with the colonists, and so Ralph Lane's company sailed with him back to England. Manteo, a Croatoan and friend of the English colonists who had traveled to England with them once before, was also on board.[12]

All the while, Sir Richard Grenville had been on his way back across the Atlantic with a supply fleet to restock the colonists. It consisted of five ships, four hundred men and ample provisions. He reached Roanoke just two weeks after Lane and his men had caught a ride back to England with Sir Francis Drake. Grenville's men went ashore to look for the colony but found their fort abandoned. The only signs of human presence they found were the bodies of an Englishman and a native that had been hanged—a mystery in its own right. It was apparent that it had not been long since their execution, judging from the grim fact that the men's bodies had not yet separated from their heads. This would have taken only several weeks during the hot summer months. Grenville didn't find any other Englishmen on the island or surrounding areas of Ossomocomuck, nor did he encounter Algonquians, who were oddly absent. They were likely hiding from the English, their numbers weakened by disease and attack. After searching for signs of life for two weeks, they did manage to capture one native who spoke enough English to tell them that Lane and his men had returned to England with Drake. Richard Grenville left fifteen of his four hundred men on Roanoke Island to "hold down the fort," as it were, with enough provisions for two years. He then sailed back to England.[13]

Making a Home in Hostile Territory

John White's 1587 colony, tasked with locating the fifteen men left behind by Richard Grenville on their way to the Chesapeake Bay, found little comfort when they came to the English fort where the men were last seen a year earlier. It had been ransacked and abandoned, overgrown with vines. Not only absent of Englishmen, the island appeared to have been deserted by the Roanoke tribe as well. The only signs of life White and his colony found were some deer feeding on melons that had grown in the underbrush and the sun-bleached skeleton of one of Grenville's men, offering a grim sign of what had happened there. This shouldn't have taken John White by surprise, as he was a part of the 1585 voyage, but it may have. As Oberg reasons:

> *That White fully expected Grenville's men to be alive suggests that he believed that the Algonquians had been badly weakened by English diseases, or that the bloody conclusion of the previous year's colonization effort posed no obstacle to good relations between natives and newcomers…* [but] *from the outset White's colonists would contend with the legacy of Lane's attack on Dasemunkepeuc.*[14]

Fourteen families, including White's expecting daughter Eleanor and his son-in-law Ananias Dare, had come on this voyage under the notion that the New World would be relatively safe and suitable for settlement. It was now frighteningly apparent that the colonists had been left in hostile territory, rendered so by their own countrymen. They set about repairing the structures in the abandoned fort and building new houses to accommodate the whole party, not knowing when the next tragedy might befall them.

It happened one week later, on July 28, when a colonist named George Howe wandered two miles from the settlement to look for crabs. He was alone and unarmed when Algonquian hunters, who had been hiding in the woods, "shot at him in the water, where they gave him sixteen wounds with their arrows and after they had slain him with their wooden swords, beat his head in pieces."[15] All the while, the colonists were unloading their supplies from the ships and preparing to make a home for themselves. The evidence suggests that Pemisapan's people were responsible for the attack and likely fled to nearby Secotan to avoid English retaliation. No large-scale attack by the natives occurred afterward.

In search of answers and allies, the colonists visited the village of Croatoan to the south, where Manteo's family and people lived. John White wrote of their encounter:

> *We hoped to understand some news of our fifteen men, but especially to learn the disposition of the people of the Country towards us, and to renew our old friendship with them. At our first landing, they seemed as though they would fight with us: but perceiving us begin to march with our shot towards them, they turned their backs and fled. Then Manteo, their countryman, called to them in their own language, whom, as soon as they heard, they returned, and threw away their bows and arrows and some of them came unto us, embracing and entertaining us friendly, desiring us not to gather or spill any of their corn, for they had but little. We answered them that neither their corn nor any other thing of theirs should be diminished by any of us, and that our coming was only to renew the old love that was between us and them at the first, and to live with them as brethren and friends.*[16]

Above all, the Croatoans wanted the English to stay away from their food supply. Judging from this encounter, they were apparently prepared to fight or feign friendship to accomplish this end. They also asked the English to give them some sort of "token or badge" so that they could be identified as friendly if the English saw them "anywhere out of the town or island." Several of their people had been mistaken for Wingina's followers and attacked by Ralph Lane's men a year earlier. The Croatoans confirmed that Grenville's fifteen men had been attacked by Pemisapan's remaining followers, but even still John White was ready to make peace. He asked the Croatoans to speak to the other villages on his behalf, "that if they would accept our friendship...all unfriendly dealings past, on both parties, should be utterly forgiven and forgotten."[17] White called a meeting set for August 8 where he and the weroances from the surrounding areas might discuss this, but when the day of the meeting arrived and no one came, he decided that getting revenge for the deaths of Grenville's men and George Howe would be the next course of action. The following day, White, Manteo and twenty-four other men went to Dasemunkepeuc to seek out their enemies. John White wrote:

> *We presently set on them* [and] *the miserable souls herewith amassed, fled into a place of thick reeds, among which we hoped to acquit their evil doing towards us, but we were deceived, for those Savages were our friends,*

Above: An engraving of John White's watercolor depicts "their manner of carrying their children and attire of the chief ladies of the town of Dasemunkepeuc," which was located near modern-day Manns Harbor. *Photo courtesy of the John Carter Brown Library.*

Right: Marjalene Thomas plays the role of Eleanor Dare, looking upon her infant, Virginia Dare, who was born on Roanoke Island in 1587. Thomas first appeared in a production of *The Lost Colony* as a child in 1938, the second year of the production. *Photo courtesy of the Outer Banks History Center, Aycock Brown Papers.*

> *and were come from Croatoan, to gather the corn and fruit of that place, because they understood our enemies were fled immediately after they had slaine George Howe.*[18]

The colonists had attacked the Croatoan people who had just been amicable enough to renew their friendship with them—the Croatoans, who had asked the English for some sort of badge to designate that they were friendly, to avoid being attacked by mistake. John White explained that "it was so dark, that they being naked, and their men and women apparelled all so like others" was the reason that they had "paid dearly"[19] and fallen victim to the colonists' surprise attack. It would seem that the English had burned all their bridges. But into the darkness came one bright new light.

VIRGINIA DARE: THE FIRST ENGLISH CHILD BORN IN THE NEW WORLD

In the sixteenth century, infant and maternal mortality rates during childbirth were high. Eleanor Dare faced the birth of her child on distant shores, far from home and every comfort she had known, but her body and her mind upheld her. She would survive the ordeal. On August 18, 1587, Eleanor gave birth to a healthy daughter. Virginia Dare is known to this day as the first English child born and baptized in the New World. She is likely the most famous female historical figure in Outer Banks lore, with a special place in all of our hearts. Perhaps the arrival of a new life, innocent and pure, offered hope amid the violence and struggle on Roanoke Island. Or perhaps it made the colonists realize the urgency of setting up a viable colony that was capable of sustaining not just the lives of soldiers but those of infants, children and the elderly and infirm.

The Algonquian people had been feeding and raising families and living among extended relatives and kinship groups for centuries, but they weren't likely to help the colonists achieve the same now. Their familial ties and tribal structure had been devastated and disrupted by their encounters with the English. While it is easy for people to attach themselves sentimentally to the infant girl born on Roanoke Island, and while the tale of the lost colonists is remarkable, we must also acknowledge the devastating effects that colonization had on the area's Indigenous people and its ripple effect into the present day.

A scene from the 1921 silent film about the "Lost Colony," depicting Eleanor Dare among the colonists as they debated John White's return to England. The film was produced by Mabel Evans Jones and directed by Elizabeth Grimball, both native North Carolinians. *Photo courtesy of the Outer Banks History Center, D. Victor Meekins Collection.*

The colonists pleaded with John White to return to England for supplies and to inform Sir Walter Raleigh of their situation. They feared revenge for their attack on Dasemunkepeuc. White, not wanting his departure from the colony to look like abandonment, strongly objected to leaving. He had just become a grandfather; the idea of leaving his granddaughter behind along with his daughter must have been devastating.

On August 25, 1587, the colonists put their request in writing so that White might have some proof that he was acting on behalf of the colony when he arrived back on English soil. He knew that the colony was planning to relocate approximately fifty miles inland,[20] and as Simon Fernando prepared the ships for their return voyage, John White and the colonists hatched a plan. The colonists agreed that if they left Roanoke Island, they would carve the name of their destination on a tree, a "secret token" to communicate their whereabouts to John White. If they left in distress, they would carve a cross over the name. With that, John White departed and sailed back to England. What happened to the colonists on Roanoke Island while he was away has captivated the world's imagination ever since.

The Lost Colony: Return to Roanoke in 1590

It wasn't until the year 1590 that John White returned to Roanoke Island. Seven men drowned while the company tried to cross into the sound from the Hatteras Inlet, but White made it through. The night of August 17, as he and his men approached the north end of Roanoke Island, where John White had last seen the colonists, they were met with a sign of hope.

> *There we spied towards the north end of the island the light of a great fire through the woods, to which we presently rowed. When we came right over against it, we let fall our* [anchor] *near the shore, and sounded with a trumpet a call, and afterwards many familiar English tunes of songs, and called to them friendly; but we had no answer. We therefore landed at day-break, and coming to the fire, we found the grass & sundry rotten trees burning about the place.*[21]

Had Eleanor Dare and little Virginia been sitting around the fire that night, the melodies of familiar English songs coming off the water would have been the perfect gift. The next day, when her grandfather finally came ashore, marked Virginia Dare's third birthday.

To his dismay, John White found the island deserted and the settlement overgrown with weeds and vines. He had buried trunks full of maps, books and drawings for safekeeping before he left and found them unearthed, their contents ruined. His most important findings, however, were the letters CRO carved into a tree and the full word CROATOAN carved into a post in the palisade "without any cross or sign of distress."[22] His hope was renewed, as this signified to him that the colonists had joined their Croatoan allies farther south on Hatteras Island—but he would never make it there. Due to bad weather and treacherous ocean conditions, he was once again forced to return to England without finding Eleanor and Virginia.

Facts and Folklore: The Uncertain Fate of the Lost Colonists

In the years since the "lost colonists" seemingly disappeared, theories as to their fate have been many. This great mystery of American history has prompted dozens of books, archaeological digs, myths and legends. The answer given in Paul Green's production of *The Lost Colony* is that the colonists either were killed by the Spanish, died in the woods or went to live with the native people and faded into history like morning fog hanging over the marsh. The "Legend of the White Doe" tells of how Virginia Dare grew into a fair maiden but, when she rejected an admirer, was turned into an immortal white doe by an act of sorcery. The legend holds that she still wanders the shores of the Outer Banks today.

Keep in mind that the "lost colonists" weren't the first group to "disappear" on Roanoke Island. It had happened twice before in the span of just three years, between 1584 and 1587. Ralph Lane's men could not be found when Richard Grenville returned to Roanoke with supplies in 1586, but a captive was able to reveal that they had sailed away with Drake. The fifteen men Richard Grenville then left behind were nowhere to be seen when John White's 1587 colony landed on Roanoke to search for them, but the Croatoan people told them of their demise. When the 1587 colonists seemingly vanished without a trace three years later, there was simply no one available or willing to answer the question of their fate.

Some historians believe that a portion of the colonists went to the village of Croatoan to live among Manteo's people, as their carvings suggested. There is anecdotal and archaeological evidence to support this. When the explorer John Lawson visited Hatteras Island in the early 1700s, he claims to have spoken with Native Americans who told him that "several of their ancestors were white people" that had blue eyes and could "talk in a book."[23] An English signet ring and other European artifacts have been unearthed on Hatteras Island to further support this claim. While some of the colonists likely migrated to Hatteras Island, anthropologists and historians believe others in the group may have gone fifty miles inland, as discussed with John White.

A curious discovery in 1937 suggests that Eleanor, Ananias and Virginia Dare were among the group that went "further into the maine." A stone weighing twenty-one pounds that appeared to have old English writing etched into it was discovered by a motorist named Louis Hammond near the Chowan River's eastern shore. The mouth of the Chowan River, near Edenton, North Carolina, is roughly sixty miles from Roanoke Island by way of modern roads. Hammond took the stone to Emory University in Atlanta, where he handed it over to Dr. Haywood Pearce.[24]

The inscription on the front of the stone read: "Ananias Dare & Virginia Went Hence Unto Heaven 1591. Any Englishman Show John White Gov Virginia."[25] While the stone's front seemed to serve the purpose of a grave

Above: Front (*left*) and rear (*right*) view of the first "Dare Stone," found in 1937. *Photos courtesy of Brenau University.*

Opposite: The Virginia Dare Monument, pictured here in the early 1900s, was dedicated in 1896. It commemorates Raleigh's colonists and the birth of Virginia Dare on Roanoke Island in 1587. *Photo courtesy of the Outer Banks History Center, D. Victor Meekins Collection.*

marker, etched into the back was a message from Eleanor Dare for her father, John White:

> *Father Soon After You Go for England We Came Hither / Only Misery & War Two Year / Above Half Dead ere Two Year More From Sickness Being Four & Twenty / Savage with Message of Ship Unto Us / Small Space of Time they Afraid of Revenge Ran All Away / We Believe it Not You / Soon After Ye Salvages Faine Spirits Angry / Sudden Murder All Save Seven / Mine Child /Ananias too Slain with Much Misery /Bury All Near Four Miles East This River Upon Small Hill / Names Writ All There On Rock / Put This There Also / Savage Show This Unto You & Hither We Promise You to Give Great Plenty Presents / EWD*

The initials EWD have been interpreted to represent Eleanor White Dare. She paints a picture of an attack by Native Americans after they spotted English ships in the waterways. All but seven of the colonists were

killed, including Virginia Dare, who would have been three or four at the time, and Eleanor's husband, Ananias. She indicates a burial ground and a gravestone four miles east of the Chowan River and offers a handsome reward to any "savage" who might find the stone and show it to the English. While the find is fascinating, many questioned the authenticity of this "Dare Stone," especially when over forty more of them showed up, scattered throughout the South. All of the Dare Stones are now housed at Brenau

University in Gainesville, Georgia, and have undergone various scientific studies. The forty-some stones found states away from the Chowan River are widely regarded as a hoax, but the original stone still holds the potential of being authentic. We may have the desperate scrawling of a bereaved mother preserved in rock, Eleanor's attempt to tell her story and leave behind clues to the mystery of the lost colony. The Choanoac people of that area were a group of Algonquians that had ties with Manteo and may have been friendly to the colonists.[26] If the Dare Stone is real, perhaps the Choanoac welcomed the colonists initially but then turned hostile. There were several precedents for this, since the English first arrived to the area in 1584. If the Dare Stone is a fraud, it may still be feasible that some of the colonists settled on the banks of the Chowan River and assimilated into Choanoac society, while the others remained at Croatoan.

We may never know. What we do know is that a woman named Eleanor Dare lived and gave life on the shores of the Carolina Sounds. She witnessed a clash of cultures, the brutality of survival and the devastation that comes from the inability to trust others. All verified accounts of her story come from other people in her life—governors, scientists and ship captains—whose reports have been sealed into the sepulcher of recorded history. As we now move forward through Outer Banks history, let this tale highlight the importance of women having the tools to tell their own stories and the freedom to chart their own course.

Chapter 2

FINDING FREEDOM

Chrissy Bowser, Late 1800s

On the north end of Roanoke Island stands an ancient oak tree that has silently borne witness to the passing of days and people across the island for centuries. It is known as the "Chrissy Oak," named for Christaina Bowser. Its mammoth trunk and sprawling branches stand vigil over her final resting place. Like her oak, Chrissy witnessed Roanoke Island before, during and after the Civil War and experienced its life-altering impact on her community.

A Long Life Marked by Mystery

Christaina "Chrissy" Bowser reportedly lived to be over 100 years old. Though her birth year was likely somewhere between 1815 and 1830, a 1914 newspaper article announcing her death on March 6 of that year reports that she was 105 years old. Espousing her longevity, the writeup claims her age was "established by authentic records." If Chrissy did live to be over one hundred, it made her the second-oldest person on Roanoke Island (after Fanny Midgett, who was supposedly 113) and likely the second-oldest person in eastern North Carolina at that time.[27] However, record-keeping for non-White persons in the antebellum period was negligible. Birth dates and names were often fluid or undocumented altogether. Chrissy is listed by various names, including "Christiana," "Chrysa," "Christia" and "Crissey," across historical records. Multiple censuses approximate 1830 as her birth

Historians believe this to be a portrait of Chrissy Bowser, or "Aunt Chrissy," circa 1910. Oral history accounts recall her sitting in front of her cabin often. The board-and-batten exterior is similar to other outbuildings that were on or near the Etheridge farm during this period. *Photo courtesy of the Outer Banks History Center, D. Victor Meekins Collection.*

year, but on her death record it is ultimately listed as 1815. This would have made her 99 years old at the time of her passing. Whether Chrissy was born free or into slavery is the biggest mystery surrounding what we know of her life. Though historical records neither confirm nor deny either scenario, we do know that she died a landowner, a remarkable accomplishment for a woman of color in early twentieth-century America. Though crucial aspects of her identity are hard to uncover, never having been captured on paper, Chrissy lived a full and fascinating life outside of lists and ledgers.

In the first half of Chrissy's long life, Roanoke Island and the Outer Banks were an isolated, predominantly White community that subsisted on fishing and some farming. Few people of color lived on the Outer Banks, but the majority of those who did were enslaved, according to census records. The enslaved population was relatively small compared to communities farther inland. While wealthy planter families kept large plantations on the mainland, most Outer Bankers saw little reason to own slaves.[28] However, it is documented that slave labor was used to tend fields, clear land, mend fishnets, care for children and carry out housework on the Outer Banks.

Alongside the enslaved, there was also a population of "free colored" people living on Roanoke Island prior to the Civil War. They were classified as either "Black" or "Mulatto" on census records, though many were also Native American. The census offers a limited view of the diverse makeup of Roanoke Island's people, who in reality were a blend of African, White European and Indigenous Algonquian descent.

Most of the "free colored" people on the island were Bowsers. The Bowser family's freedom can be traced back to our country's colonial period, when, in 1676, an enslaved man in Virginia named Anthony Bowser petitioned for his freedom. He was referred to as "Tony Bowze Negro" in the records of the Virginia General Court, which detail how he produced a document written in his late master's hand mandating that Anthony was to pay eight hundred pounds of tobacco yearly in exchange for his freedom. Determining the letter to be authentic, the court ruled in Anthony's favor, and he was granted his freedom.[29]

A reproduction of a slave cabin at Island Farm, which interprets life on the Etheridge homestead circa 1850. It resembles the building Chrissy Bowser is seated in front of in her portrait. *Photo courtesy of Lauren Cowart.*

As far back as the year 1800, we find documentation of the Bowser family, who may have been descendants of Anthony Bowser, living as free people on the Outer Banks.[30] According to the Algonquian Indians of North Carolina, Inc., the "Bowser Town" area of Roanoke Island was once an Indian descendants' community.[31] The Bowsers, along with the Berrys, Daniels, Pughs and Westcotts (to name a few), are among the Outer Banks families who claim Native American ancestry, illustrating the blending of Black, White and Indigenous people in the area and contributing to the diverse heritage shared by Outer Bankers today.

Uncovering the Origins of Chrissy Bowser

The 1860 Federal Census reports approximately 171 slaves and twenty-four free Black or Mulatto people living on Roanoke Island in that year, mostly on the North End. However, enslaved people were not named in census records, only numbered in the households of their slaveholders. Of the twenty-four "free colored" individuals who were named, nineteen of them were Bowsers. Only nine of these Bowsers lived in their own residences (in three separate homes), and the rest lived in the homes of their White employers, where they worked as farm laborers or servants and where each of them was the only non-White person in the residence.[32] This data reveals that, despite their status as free people, non-White people still found themselves largely dependent on Whites for income and housing. Furthermore, this dependence disrupted their ability to live together as families or in multigenerational households, distancing loved ones much like slavery did.

The relationship between all of the free Bowsers on this census isn't entirely known, but the likelihood of their kinship in the small, isolated community is high. However, Chrissy was not listed among them. She first appears in the 1870 census, listed as Christaina Bowser.[33] She was working as a domestic servant in the household of Peter G. Gallop, who also happened to be the census taker that year. The 1870 census is significant for several reasons: it was the first census taken after the Civil War, the first taken in the newly formed Dare County[34] and the first to name all people of color—including former slaves—since slavery was abolished by the Thirteenth Amendment in 1865. Chrissy's absence from antebellum census records could indicate that she was enslaved at the time, since enslaved persons were only numbered in the households of their masters and not named. There is also likelihood that she may have been a "free colored" person listed under another name prior to 1870 or missed by population schedules for other reasons, which was not unheard of. In fact, we know population schedules to be rife with inaccuracies. Chrissy's information on the 1870 census contains several errors when compared with her records on subsequent censuses. She is recorded in 1870 as being fifty-eight years old, but in 1880 she is listed as fifty.[35] This is likely due to the uncertainty of her birth year, which may point to enslavement. Chrissy may have been deprived of the ceremony and celebration of marking birthdays as a child. This was a painful reality for many African Americans who were born into slavery. In his first autobiography, *Narrative of the Life of Frederick Douglass*, the famous abolitionist wrote:

> *I have no accurate knowledge of my age, never having seen any authentic record containing it. By far the larger part of the slaves know as little of their ages as horses know of theirs, and it is the wish of most masters within my knowledge to keep their slaves thus ignorant. I do not remember to have ever met a slave who could tell of his birthday....A want of information concerning my own was a source of unhappiness to me even during childhood. The white children could tell their ages. I could not tell why I ought to be deprived of the same privilege. I was not allowed to make any inquiries of my master concerning it. He deemed all such inquiries on the part of a slave improper and impertinent, and evidence of a restless spirit.*[36]

Another error on Chrissy's first census record is that her race was listed as White, puzzling due to the fact that she was living in the household of the census taker. However, the race category on census records was often mutable for people of color in this period. Marilyn Berry Morrison, chief of the Roanoke-Hatteras tribe of the Algonquian Indians of North Carolina today, succinctly points out that "the records are not correct" in an article by Corinne Saunders for the North Carolina Coastal Federation. Morrison's family members and ancestors are alternatingly listed as Black, White and Mulatto across different censuses, marriage records and other official documents,[37] while their Native American identity is overlooked. Family and oral history was likely the best record-keeper of racial identity; on paper it could be misrepresented, oversimplified or effectively erased.

Our history lessons often portray Native Americans as a people who once lived here but were then killed or relocated, mythicizing their culture. To honor and bring awareness to the Indigenous lineage that still runs through Roanoke Island, Marilyn took part in a project placing blue, yellow and

This portrait of Annie Mariah Simmons Pugh, taken on Roanoke Island in 1915, hangs in the National Museum of the American Indian. She is the great-great-grandmother of Marilyn Berry Morrison, chief of the Roanoke-Hatteras tribe of the Algonquian Indians of North Carolina. Many descendants of indigenous Algonquians still live on the Outer Banks today. *Photo courtesy of the National Museum of the American Indian, Smithsonian Institution.*

white flags on the graves of people with Native American heritage at several local churches, including Haven Creek Baptist Church, established during the Civil War. "Our people are still here; they never left," says the chief. "They are home on Roanoke Island." The Roanoke-Croatoan tribe is still working toward recognition as an official North Carolina tribe, after applying over a decade ago.[38]

In 1870, Chrissy was one of just three Bowsers living in the home of a White employer. In stark contrast to the previous decade, the majority of the Bowser family (twenty-three individuals on the census) now resided in their own homes, living under the same roof with immediate and extended family members.[39] The changes brought by the Civil War appear to have altered where and how family groups within the African American community lived, even among the population that was free prior to the war.

Chrissy appears to have found more autonomy as the years passed. In 1880, she was living alone in her own home and keeping a small farm for cash rental. On her two-acre plot she kept one pig and four chickens, an operation that was valued at fifty dollars, according to that years' agricultural schedule.[40] We have no way of knowing the backstory, but Dare County marriage records from 1879 list Chrissy as the mother of a groom named David Bowser. A man named Thomas Hill is named as his father.[41] Neither Chrissy nor David nor Thomas are named in any census records until after the Civil War, suggesting they may have come from a different area or that they may have all been enslaved. Perhaps Chrissy and Thomas lived together on a slaveholder's property when they had their child. The nuances of their relationship are unknown, as unions or marriages between enslaved persons had no legal status at the time. However, it appears that Chrissy's son David was given her last name, and when Chrissy begins to show up in census records starting in 1870, she

Five generations of the Wise and Barber families of Roanoke Island pose together for a photo. The number of Black heads of household increased after the Civil War as more people began living together in multigenerational family settings rather than in the homes of White employers. *Photo courtesy of the Outer Banks History Center, D. Victor Meekins Collection.*

is listed as single. David was twenty-five years old and living in a separate household. Thomas is not listed as a resident of the island, an indicator that he was likely among the hundreds of freed slaves who left the area after the Freedmen's Colony was dispersed in 1867.[42]

Finding Safe Haven on Roanoke Island

Formed by the Union army in 1862, the Roanoke Island Freedmen's Colony provided refuge to over three thousand former slaves at its height, though no complete rosters of the individuals who lived in the colony were kept. The Freedmen were made up of formerly enslaved Roanoke Island residents, but the vast majority came from plantations in surrounding areas of eastern North Carolina.[43] The colony had a school, several churches and over five hundred homes, providing former slaves with jobs, community and liberation at long last. When the U.S. government began shutting down the camps several years later, ordering that the land be returned to its original owners, a group of Freedmen appealed for an extension:

> *The undersigned colored citizens of Roanoke Island N.C. having received orders to remove from the lands of I.C. Meekins and others respectfully request a short extension of time. It being midwinter and having to be thrown out without shelter, our suffering must be very great. Also the season for Shad fishing, an occupation which we nearly all follow for a living comes in direct conflict with said order we being constantly engaged in filling our nets, boats, &c. If in your judgement you can show us a little leniency and give us till the middle of May or the first of June next, we promise faithfully and pledge ourselves to vacate every foot of said lands by that time.*[44]

Both the names David Bowser and Thomas Hill appear among the signatures on this 1867 letter, along with that of famed Lifesaver and fellow Freedman Richard Etheridge. It would seem that women, enslaved or not, had fewer opportunities to write their names in the pages of history, but if her son and his father were among those who signed the letter, we could presume that Chrissy Bowser was a member of the groundbreaking Freedmen's Colony as well. Ultimately, all but three hundred African Americans left Roanoke Island after the settlement was dispersed, Thomas Hill among them. As the community that sheltered the Freedmen became another of Roanoke Island's lost colonies, most of those who remained settled in a neighborhood known as California. This area was established by eleven Freedmen families that came together to purchase the land, and many of their descendants still live there today.[45]

A group of Freedpeople on St. Helena Island, South Carolina. After escaping slavery, people could at long last live together with their families, attend school and worship at Freedmen's colonies throughout the South. *Photo courtesy of the Library of Congress.*

Kith and Kin: Chrissy and the Etheridge Family

There were at least one hundred Black households on Roanoke Island by 1900, and roughly 65 percent of them were owned rather than rented.[46] Chrissy was among both the small number of Black female heads of household and the even smaller number within this group of women who owned their homes outright, with no mortgage or debt. For an unmarried woman of color, these accomplishments were nothing short of revolutionary. Chrissy Bowser had a home, land and livelihood after starting life without so much as a birth date.

Chrissy lived near the Etheridges, a prominent and deep-rooted White family on the island. Through research and preservation conducted by the Outer Banks Conservationists, a significant amount is known about the Etheridge family and their farmstead. Fully restored and operating today as a living history site known as Island Farm, the property provides a glimpse into the daily lives of a family who lived, worked and had a close relationship with Chrissy Bowser.

Adam Dough Etheridge, born in 1813, built his "mansion house" on the north end of Roanoke Island sometime between 1845 and 1852. Built on a twenty-acre farmstead deeded to him by his father, the house is a two-story timber-frame dwelling built of heart pine and cypress. Its front and rear covered porches served as additional spaces to live and work and were an integral part of family life. Inside, the whitewashed walls were neither insulated nor plastered, and the windows were small; there was one chimney and evidence of a detached kitchen. Though bare and utilitarian by today's standards, the Etheridge homeplace was large and relatively elaborate in terms of nineteenth-century architecture on Roanoke Island: a mansion indeed.

The building style and layout of Adam Dough Etheridge's "mansion house" was similar to that of the Meekins homeplace on Roanoke Island, pictured here circa 1915. *Photo courtesy of the Outer Banks History Center, D. Victor Meekins Collection.*

The Etheridge family farmhouse today, restored to its appearance circa 1850 by the Outer Banks Conservationists. *Photo courtesy of Lauren Cowart.*

Adam and his wife, Fannie Baum Etheridge, raised six children under their roof. They labored, along with their five slaves, to raise livestock, produce wool, churn butter and grow corn, peas, beans, Irish potatoes and sweet potatoes. Outbuildings on the property would have included stables, a dairy, a cookhouse and a slave house. In terms of their farmstead's buildings and possessions, they were a wealthy Roanoke Island family.[47]

When the flames of the Civil War spread to North Carolina's sandy shores and General Ambrose Burnside captured Roanoke Island in 1862, Adam Dough Etheridge took an oath of allegiance to the Union army along with his brother, John B. Etheridge.[48] Adam was able to keep his house and most of his farm, though some of his neighbors weren't as fortunate. To the northeast of the Etheridge farm, the Mann house was converted into a hospital during the battle, while another neighboring home served as Burnside's headquarters. While the land of other local farmers was appropriated for the Freedmen's Colony settlement, Etheridge's was not.[49] His five slaves are assumed to have quit his farm during the occupation and likely joined their fellow "contrabands" in the colony, finding their first taste of freedom.[50] Perhaps here they waved to Chrissy in the street, nodded along with her at meetings or sat next to her in a church pew. Perhaps they were members of her own

Union troops, aided by local enslaved informants, were able to navigate from their position on Hatteras Island and land on Roanoke Island in 1862, easily defeating Confederate forces that were left vulnerable to attack. *Photo courtesy of the Outer Banks History Center.*

extended family, reunited. A sixteen-year-old Vicy Bowser and her brother William Bowser (fourteen) are listed as free Mulatto dependents in the home of Adam Etheridge III in 1850. The suggestion is that Adam III may have fathered the two Bowser children with a Black woman in his household. Adam was also the father of Adam Dough Etheridge, whom Chrissy lived near and cooked for. His children called her "Aunt Chrissy." Could Adam's half sister Vicy Bowser actually be Chrissy Bowser, indeed making her an aunt to his children? It may not be possible to uncover the answer.[51] Neither Vicy nor Chrissy are found on the 1860 census.

We do know that from sometime in the late 1800s until the early 1900s, "Aunt Chrissy" continued to live alone near the Etheridge farm while working as a cook for the family. When Adam Dough Etheridge died, she continued to cook for Fannie Etheridge and her second husband, Thomas Dough, and later for Fannie's youngest son, Augustus Etheridge. A wedding reception for Augustus and his bride was held at the homeplace in 1888, and he recalled "Aunt Chrissy, our colored cook" helping his mother prepare dinner for the party.[52] Despite her life's hardships, Chrissy "was

Left: Portrait of Augustus H. Etheridge circa 1900. He remembered Chrissy Bowser fondly as "Aunt Chrissy" and saw that she was cared for into her old age. *Photo courtesy of the Outer Banks Conservationists Collection.*

Right: A portrait of Frances "Fannie" Etheridge Dough (1826–94). Chrissy Bowser worked as a cook alongside Fannie at the Etheridge homestead. *Photo courtesy of the Outer Banks Conservationists Collection.*

famous for her sunny, genial disposition" and "inexhaustive stock of stories of antebellum days with which she entertained her visitors."[53] If only these stories had been recorded.

In the last years of Chrissy's life, Augustus "looked after her and saw that she lacked for nothing."[54] Sometime after 1910, she moved into a simple board-and-batten cabin on the Etheridge farm. Family history remembers Chrissy sitting on the front stoop of her cabin, barring the entrance with her outstretched legs and "from what could be seen from the door she apparently had little furniture and no bed."[55] Chrissy Bowser lived quietly on the farm until her death in 1914. On the day of her death, in early March, she was laid out in one of the Etheridges' storehouses, where family and friends could pay their last respects, then buried under the ancient tree still known to this day as the "Chrissy Oak."[56]

The Civil War brought major upheaval to the lives of White and Black Outer Bankers alike, and while the tendrils of racial tension are still being

Chrissy Bowser was laid to rest under an ancient oak tree on the north end of Roanoke Island known as the "Chrissy Oak." It resembles the massive oak, pictured here, on the nearby Island Farm property where she once lived and worked. *Photo courtesy of Lauren Cowart.*

teased out in modern times, a sturdy North End oak memorializing the life of Chrissy Bowser reminds us of our shared history and the power of perseverance on these isolated barrier islands where her descendants still walk.

Chapter 3

WELCOMING THE WRIGHT BROTHERS

Irene Tate, Early 1900s

On the morning of September 12, 1900, there was an unexpected knock on the door of the Tate family's Kitty Hawk residence. They answered it to find their neighbor boy, Elijah Baum, standing with a "strange gentleman" who looked travel-worn and weary. The stranger took off his cap and introduced himself as Wilbur Wright from Dayton, Ohio.[57] Little did the Tates know that the man they had just received would become world famous, along with his brother Orville, for humankind's first flight.

Destined for Flight

Irene Tate, born in 1897, was just three years old when Wilbur arrived at her family home, but the impact of his visit influenced the course of her life. As fate would have it, she was destined to take to the sky herself, becoming the first female pilot to fly round trip from New York to Miami.[58]

A month prior to Wilbur's arrival on their doorstep, Irene's father, Captain William Tate, was asked by the Weather Bureau to respond to a letter that Wilbur had sent, inquiring about the wind conditions on the Outer Banks. The weatherman was ready to toss the letter into the wastebasket, citing that it was from "some damn fool who wants to fly a kite that'll carry a man."[59] Bill Tate, reading the letter and deciding that Wilbur was no fool, wrote in reply:

> *The Weather Bureau here has asked me to answer your letter…relative to the fitness of Kitty Hawk as a place to practice or experiment with a flying machine, etc.…In answering I would say that you would find here nearly any type of ground you could wish…our winds are always steady, generally from 10 to 20 miles velocity per hour.…If you decide to try your machine here and come, I will take pleasure in doing all I can for your convenience and success and pleasure, and I assure you will find a hospitable people when you come among us.*[60]

Bill advised that they visit no later in the season than October and that Kitty Hawk could be reached by boat from Elizabeth City (thirty-five miles away) or by mail boat from Manteo (twelve miles away) every Monday, Wednesday and Friday. He provided no other specifics on how to reach them. Regardless, this convinced the Wright brothers to settle on Kitty Hawk for their experiments. It had the weather conditions and the seclusion that they sought, with the

The Tate family circa 1900, seated on the front porch of their home, which also served as the Kitty Hawk post office. Irene is seated on the lap of her father, Captain William "Bill" Tate. Her sister, Pauline, stands by their mother, Addie Tate, and a neighbor. *Photo courtesy of Special Collections and Archives, Wright State University.*

promise of southern hospitality to boot. Wilbur either overlooked the need to write back or just didn't bother and instead made preparations for the long trip from Dayton, showing up in Kitty Hawk unannounced on that September morning.[61]

Irene Tate (*left*) pictured with her brother Elijah (*standing*) and sister, Pauline (*right*), circa 1915. Not pictured is the youngest Tate sibling, Lewis. *Photo courtesy of Tammi Pittaro.*

In 1900, the Tate family lived on present-day Moor Shore Road in a simple two-story wooden house that doubled as the Kitty Hawk post office. Irene's mother, Addie Tate, served as the postmistress and Irene's father, Captain Tate, as assistant postmaster. Irene's sister, Pauline, was a year younger, and the family would later welcome two sons, Elijah and Lewis. Their home was unpainted and rudimentary by Dayton standards but above average for Kitty Hawk. When the family invited Wilbur into their home that September morning, he proceeded to tell them of his struggle to reach the Outer Banks from Elizabeth City—"He was a tenderfoot and of course had a tale of woe to tell," Captain Tate would later write—and that he had eaten nothing for the past forty-eight hours except a jar of jelly that his sister Katherine had slipped into his suitcase for the journey. Hearing this, Addie prepared a breakfast of coffee, ham and fresh eggs for their guest.[62]

In a letter home to his father, Wilbur wrote that the house had "no carpets at all, very little furniture, no books or pictures" and no plaster on the walls. Yet overhearing Addie's private hesitations about boarding him, Wilbur assured the Tates that he would be thankful for any accommodations they could offer until his brother arrived to help him set up camp elsewhere.[63] The Tate house is no longer standing, but a stone marker has been erected in its place commemorating the location's connection to the Wrights. It reads:

> *On this spot Sept. 17, 1900 Wilbur Wright began the assembly of the Wright Brothers' first experimental glider which led to man's conquest of the air.*

The Tate home in 1927, where Wilbur Wright stayed for part of his first trip to the Outer Banks in 1900. Here he assembled his and Orville's experimental glider in the front yard. *Photo courtesy of Special Collections and Archives, Wright State University.*

"A DARN FOOL CONTRAPTION": LOCALS EMBRACE THE WRIGHT BROTHERS DESPITE THEIR APPREHENSION

Moor Shore Road today is a scenic, wooded road that follows the gentle curve of Kitty Hawk Bay. It is only around a half-mile long and seldom used, except by locals avoiding summer traffic and as part of the Outer Banks Marathon route. In the year 1900, it connected the Tates' home and post office in the village of Kitty Hawk to present-day Kill Devil Hills and Nags Head. On that seventeenth day of September, the Wrights' flying machine "paraphernalia" was brought to the Tate home after arriving on the weekly freight boat from Elizabeth City. Wilbur wasted no time in getting started on their project while awaiting Orville Wright's arrival. He began assembling the glider made of wooden ribs and sheaths of cloth in the Tates' front yard, where a young Irene was a curious onlooker.

Initially, the odd invention frightened her. "I can distinctly remember I had seen a dead cow when I was [a child] walking through the woods with my father," she recalled as an adult. "This thing reminded me of something dead and it terrified me."[64] She wasn't the only local wary of Wilbur's undertaking. According to Captain Tate:

We natives got curious and began to discuss him and his darn fool contraption that he was sewing, glueing, and tying together with string. In the meantime, it had been drawn out of him by adroit questioning that his brother would be down in a couple of weeks, they were going to live in a tent and were going to make some experiments with their contraption in the art of flying. Immediately it became public information that he was inventing a flying machine, and of course all the various and sundry comments were indulged in whenever two or more natives were gathered together. If comment and criticism had been a helping factor the Wrights would have flown soon after their arrival at Kitty Hawk.[65]

Local gossip remains a powerful force in this relatively isolated community. To provide context to the criticism of the Wrights' work when reflecting on it years later, Captain William Tate thought it necessary for people to understand the perspective of Kitty Hawkers at the time. He described them as a "hardy race" of people who were mostly the descendants of shipwreck survivors; he himself was the son of a shipwrecked Scotsman. They had

Orville and Wilbur Wright (*right*) complete the world's first powered, controlled, sustained flight in Kitty Hawk, North Carolina, on December 17, 1903. *Photo courtesy of the Library of Congress.*

limited access to formal education, battled with the sea for subsistence, had few transportation options and were "out of touch" with the outside world. "Therefore, at the time the Wrights arrived in our community, we were set in our ways," he explained. "We believed in a good God, a bad Devil, and a hot Hell, and more than anything else we believed that the same good God did not intend man should ever fly."[66] However, he defended the locals' viewpoint by noting that before (and even after) the Wrights' first successful flight in 1903, some of the world's most brilliant and scientific minds had asserted the same.[67]

Despite their initial naysaying, the local community played an integral role in the Wrights' success. Due to the scarcity of resources in the area, Wilbur had been unable to find the spruce spars needed for the glider's design in either Norfolk or Elizabeth City and had to settle with shorter pine spars instead. As a result, one of his first hurdles was to reduce the wingspan of the glider from eighteen to seventeen feet.[68] This meant altering the wing fabric

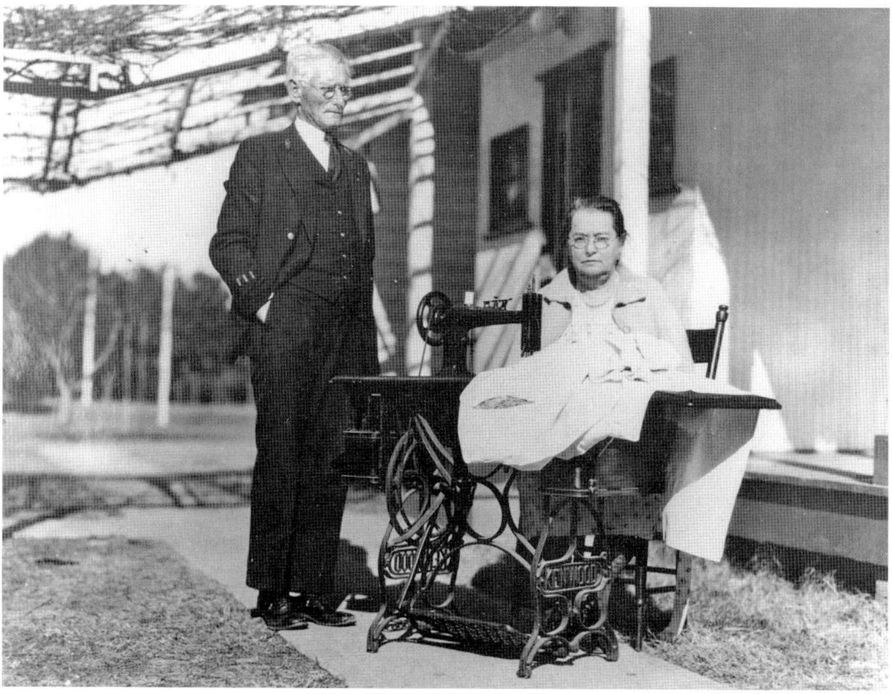

Addie Tate (*seated*) and her husband, Captain William Tate, pose with her Kenwood sewing machine circa late 1920s or 1930s. Wilbur Wright famously borrowed her machine to alter the wings for the brothers' 1900 glider. Addie's sewing machine is now on display at the Wright Brothers National Memorial visitor center. *Photo courtesy of the National Park Service, Wright Brothers National Memorial.*

Visiting from the Outer Banks circa 1920, Pauline Tate (*left*) embraces her older sister, Irene Tate Severn (*right*), on a set of steps in Atlantic City, New Jersey. The sisters were three and four years old when the Wright brothers first arrived on the Outer Banks in 1900 and befriended their family. *Photo courtesy of Tammi Pittaro.*

as well, a task for which he borrowed Addie Tate's 1899 Kenwood sewing machine, pumped by foot. It was this contribution, and many other acts of love and labor by the Tates and their fellow Outer Bankers, that aided the Wright brothers in achieving their legendary success in aviation.

When the brothers returned home to Dayton in late October 1900 after their successful first expedition to Kitty Hawk, they left the glider behind and told the Tates that they were welcome to use the materials for anything they needed. Using the same sewing machine that she lent to Wilbur, Addie Tate sewed dresses for her two little girls from the wing fabric, an imported white French sateen.[69] In a 1934 newspaper interview, Irene remembered her dress fondly as having "funny little ruffles all over the sleeves" and thought that her mother might still have some scraps of the material. She received several letters from government authorities looking for information on it. "We didn't think it would ever be of any importance," she said, explaining that the dresses had worn out and been discarded.[70] But for a time, she and her sister, descendants of shipwrecked sailors living in a community where floors were scrubbed clean with sand and people owned two to three changes of clothes at most, wore sateen dresses that had touched the sky.

OUT OF THE BLUE: IRENE MEETS BENNETT SEVERN

Sixteen years later, fate would bring another stranger to the Tate home and steer Irene one step closer to her destiny. He arrived by air, in a plane that would not have existed were it not for the Wright brothers' trip to the same salty strip of land years earlier. In January 1916, seaplane pilot Bennett D. Severn was en route from New Jersey to Palm Beach, Florida, when his aircraft burned out an engine bearing.[71] He came in low over the Currituck Sound and executed an emergency landing to bring his damaged plane down by Currituck's Long Point Lighthouse, where Captain William Tate was keeper at the time.[72] Bennett and several colleagues, including fellow pilot Edwin Jaquith, had been attempting the maiden voyage of his Curtiss F-boat down the East Coast to Florida, where he planned to conduct sightseeing tours in the off-season, as he did with tourists in Atlantic City during the summer.[73]

Ever hospitable, Captain Tate invited the downed airmen to stay in his home while they waited on engine parts to repair the plane. Nineteen-year-old Irene was introduced to the rugged pilot, and a mutual attraction began. Irene had attended nursing school in Norfolk, Virginia, and she was well

The Severns' Aeromarine flying boat lies in a crumpled heap after a crash in Atlantic City, New Jersey, with curious onlookers. Writing on the back of the photo reads: "This is one we cracked up in Atlantic City." *Photo courtesy of Tammi Pittaro.*

Irene Tate Severn (*right*) with her husband, Bennett Severn (*center*), and sister, Pauline Tate (*left*), posing in front of the couple's seaplane in Atlantic City, New Jersey, circa 1920. The sisters are wearing swimsuits sewn by their mother, Addie Tate, who also sewed them dresses from the excess wing fabric of the first Wright glider when they were little girls. *Photo courtesy of Tammi Pittaro.*

educated. Bennett was struck by her intelligence and her beauty. He was in awe that she had known the Wright brothers before they were famous, witnessed them assemble their glider in her front yard and worn dresses made of their wing fabric. The other men continued on to Florida after the plane was repaired, but Bennett Severn stayed on the island to pursue a relationship with Irene,[74] a love story that had played out in her family line once before.

Like the downed seaplane pilot, Irene's paternal grandfather, William D. Tate (the shipwrecked Scotsman), had also come to the Outer Banks under perilous circumstances when the ship he captained ran aground on the notorious Diamond Shoals. He was rescued by breeches buoy and brought ashore. There he met a beautiful young girl named Sophia, who would become Irene's grandmother. In Irene's words, "She was so pretty he kept going back. But she was too young. Her family was of English ancestry and beautiful blondes." William returned to the Outer Banks regularly until Sophia was twenty-one and agreed to marry him. They made a home in Kitty Hawk and welcomed the birth of Irene's father in 1870.[75]

Lured by a lovely siren of his own, Bennett, too, made several return trips to the Outer Banks during his courtship with Irene Tate. He was described as "good natured and affable," an athletic type who was "strong, well-built and fine-looking."[76] As America entered World War I, he was falsely accused of espionage and briefly arrested by Norfolk authorities, but Captain Tate quickly cleared his name and secured his release. In a union that seemed written in the stars, Bennett Severn and Irene Tate were married on April 28, 1917, at the Coinjock Baptist Church in Currituck County.[77]

The newlyweds left the Outer Banks for Philadelphia, where Bennett was stationed at the navy yard until the end of World War I, then settled in the small seaside town of Brigantine, New Jersey, located on a quiet island north of the glitz and bustle of Atlantic City.

A Life of Ambition and Adventure

Irene designed their family home on the water in Brigantine and acted as foreman on the construction site. True to an authentic Outer Banks tradition of salvaging, she incorporated into the home's design a staircase and some porthole windows that came from a wrecked Italian ocean liner.

A postcard featuring a seaplane belonging to Edwin Jaquith in Atlantic City, New Jersey. A fellow pilot and friend of Bennett Severn, Jaquith was considered a pioneer of the Curtiss flying boats and was with Severn on his unexpected detour to the Outer Banks in 1916. *Photo courtesy of Tammi Pittaro.*

Bennett Severn carrying a passenger through shallow water from his two-seater Aeromarine flying boat. This model appears to be the Aeromarine 40F. Primarily used by the U.S. Navy, there were only fifty ever built. *Photo courtesy of Tammi Pittaro.*

The ship's mahogany paneling was used to make dining room furniture. The enterprising couple ran a clamming business and a bait shop and service station on Brigantine Boulevard. They also operated a hotel, whose fireplace contained granite given to Irene from the monument erected in 1932 at the Wright Brothers Memorial, as well as a ballast stone fabled to have come from Sir Walter Raleigh's first expedition to Roanoke Island.[78] The spirit of her native Outer Banks imbued her hearth and home up north.

Perhaps most memorably, the couple were barnstormers. Barnstorming involved taking people on airplane rides for a small fee and/or performing aerial stunts over different small towns. The attractive, adventurous husband-and-wife duo dazzled tourists by taking them up in their plane for sightseeing tours above the coast. "In those days women were afraid of flying," said Irene. "But I used to tell them 'Look, I'm not scared to go up' and they'd get into the plane."[79]

Barnstorming was a way for airmen who had served in World War I to make a living flying postwar. For Irene, it was a way to see more of what the world had to offer. According to Tammi Pittaro, the granddaughter of Irene and Bennett, "They had quite the adventure during those early days of aviation and my grandmother was enthralled by the big world she got to see with her own eyes."

FIRST IN FLIGHT: IRENE SETS A RECORD FOR WOMEN IN AVIATION

In fulfillment of her destiny, Irene took flying lessons and became a pilot herself. In a time when there were only a handful of female aviators, she logged over fifty thousand miles in the air and became the first woman to fly round trip between New York and Miami.[80] Her first time in an airplane predates that of the famed Amelia Earhart, who was born in the same year and went up for her first ride in 1920.[81] Irene's accomplishments were only fitting for a woman who witnessed the conception and birth of aviation in her front yard and "wore the world's first wings."[82] Irene was fond of the Wright brothers and described them as "very quiet spoken men." She recalled later what they told her as a child:

> *Orville prophesied that by the time I grew up the air would be full of flying machines. Father laughed at him and said it would never be, but I've lived to see it and I've been up hundreds of times myself.* [Father] *lived long enough to know he was wrong.*[83]

After answering that knock on the door from the world's first airplane pilots, Captain William Tate experienced his own first flight with his daughter and son-in-law in 1918, when they took him up in their plane. Irene took great pride in her father's role as a lifelong friend of the Wrights and his efforts to commemorate their accomplishments on the Outer Banks. He advocated for a granite marker (and later a monument) erected at the site of their famous first heavier-than-air flight, an event which both Orville and Amelia Earhart attended in 1928.

The timeline of Irene's life became inextricably linked to the timeline of advancements in aviation throughout the years. She was the chair of the Women's Division of the National Aeronautic Association, and she was a featured speaker at National Aviation Day luncheons, held at Haddon Hall in Atlantic City, throughout the 1930s. Irene was interviewed for radio broadcasts, recounting her memories of the Wright brothers and the early days of flight just three decades prior. Postcards depicting the Wright Memorial Beacon (completed in 1932) were handed out as souvenirs, with sand from the shores of Irene's native Kitty Hawk affixed to them.

In 1961, Irene attended the commissioning of the navy's newest aircraft carrier, the *Kitty Hawk*, at the Philadelphia Navy Yard. Her sister, Pauline, was in attendance as well. Their parents, beloved natives of the carrier's

Irene Tate Severn stands with her father, Captain William Tate, by the First Flight boulder in 1938. The granite marker was dedicated in 1928 and marks the approximate liftoff point of the famous first flight completed in 1903. *Photo courtesy of Special Collections and Archives, Wright State University.*

namesake, had passed away just several years prior. Bennett, her husband and partner in both adventure and business, passed in 1965. He was well known in Brigantine for his "great booming voice" and remembered as a great conversationalist who was well traveled and well read.[84]

Irene continued to live in their home in Brigantine into her later years, keeping a menagerie of pets as her companions. "She loved animals of all kinds and kept them in pens outside—dogs, cats, rabbits, peacocks and geese," remembers her granddaughter, Tammi. "Feeding and changing their bedding took up much of her time. She insisted on cooking special food for each animal. It's safe to say that she became more and more eccentric as she aged and lived in that big house alone." Irene's prize pet was a rescued seagull named Squawker, who lived in her kitchen. "Squawker was loud and messy and required our frequent trips to the supermarket to buy him frozen smelts. She dearly loved that bird."[85]

OUTER BANKS TO OUTER SPACE: IRENE BEARS WITNESS TO THE EVOLUTION OF FLIGHT

In 1981, through the haze of old age, Irene watched the televised launch of the world's first space shuttle. Two days later, *Columbia* reentered the Earth's atmosphere and landed like a glider in the California desert. The Wright glider landing on the sandy hills of Kitty Hawk had paved the way. "The brothers would have enjoyed watching that," she remarked at age eighty-four.[86] Irene Tate Severn witnessed the world's first airplane flying over the sands of her birthplace and the world's first space shuttle launching into orbit. The two groundbreaking events in human history bookended her colorful life.

In 2020, a piece of the wing fabric from the Wright brothers' famous 1903 glider began its journey to the surface of Mars. Tucked under the solar panel of the Mars helicopter *Ingenuity*, the square of fabric is no bigger than a postage stamp, but the significance it holds for humankind is profound. It is a relic from the first powered, controlled flight on Earth and a reminder of our potential as we attempt the first powered, controlled flight on another planet. Irene would have enjoyed watching that.

Chapter 4

COLLECTING HISTORY

Nellie Myrtle Pridgen, 1940s

The image of a woman striding alone on the seashore is called to mind at the mention of Nellie Myrtle Pridgen by anyone who knew her. The sight of her lean figure, slightly stooped like a stalk of sea oats, habitually combing the stretch of sand in front of her Nags Head home was as constant and reliable as the rise and fall of the tide for nearly seven decades. The beachcomber's collection of sea-spit treasures is a record of her life's story and a cross section of Outer Banks and American history stretching back through the ages. Through collecting, she created and preserved a world that suited her during a time of rapid change in her surroundings. It was a world closely tied to the sea and her island home, to which she was fiercely devoted.

The Constant Beachcomber

Nellie Myrtle would set out every day at dawn and then again at dusk. She had a hard glamour about her. Dressed smartly in pants that hit above the ankle, wearing a coat of lipstick, with a plastic bag in hand for her finds, Nellie Myrtle combed the mile-long stretch of beach across from her residence at milepost 13 in Nags Head. She kept up the habit, really more of a ritual, for sixty years. In a true expression of her self-reliance, Nellie Myrtle purchased bolts of plastic from the hardware store to stitch together her own plastic bags before they were ever commercially available. The paper bags of the day were no match for anything heavy or wet. The expanse of sand and shell beds she walked offered up a myriad of artifacts that had been tumbled around and released by the ocean.

Nellie Myrtle picked up everything from sea glass, shells and coral to smooth, salt-tumbled bricks and driftwood. She amassed an impressive collection of lightning-struck sand, known as fulgurite, with one specimen even garnering the interest of the Smithsonian. Along with natural artifacts, man-made curiosities were often part of her haul as well: fragments of china, glass bottles, parts of porcelain dolls and other children's toys, World War II K-rations and German military helmets. On occasion, she would make the grim discovery of a bloated body that had washed ashore after a torpedo attack during the war.

Nellie Myrtle Pridgen in sunglasses and a string of pearls, probably taken around 1950. *Photo courtesy of the Nellie Myrtle Pridgen Beachcomber Collection.*

The dunes flanking Nell's combing grounds were dotted with the hulking figures of the "Unpainted Aristocracy," a group of summer cottages that comprise what is now Nags Head's historic Cottage Row District. The cottages were built by wealthy planters from the Albemarle region looking to escape the stifling heat of their inland farms during the summer. Cedar shake siding, wraparound porches, hip roofs and wooden shutters to protect from battering winds and hurricanes were hallmarks of the homes' rustic elegance. This building style was first seen around 1830 in the cottages dotting the soundside.[87]

There were few structures on the ocean side until closer to the 1950s, due to harsh weather conditions and relentless nor'easters. While summertime visitors stayed on the oceanfront, year-round residents kept to the more protected back side of the barrier island in the villages of Kitty Hawk, Colington and Nags Head Woods. This is where Nellie Myrtle's story began.

OUT OF THE WOODS: NELLIE'S EARLY LIFE

As far back as the eighteenth century, an early pocket of Outer Bankers lived in Nags Head Woods in a surprisingly thriving and self-sufficient community for its isolated location. It was nestled in a patch of maritime forest that lies between Jockey's Ridge to the south and Run Hill to the north. The large dunes buffered the village from battering winds and weather. In its heyday, the Nags Head Woods community boasted over a dozen homesteads, two churches, a school, a store and even a shingle factory and gristmill, according to the Nature Conservancy, the nonprofit organization that now maintains the preserve.[88]

Hiking the trails of the Nags Head Woods nature preserve today, you would never know you were walking the streets of a ghost town. Save for a few family cemeteries and pieces of brick foundation lying in the underbrush, nature has reclaimed the area so well that the ghosts hardly reveal themselves. High ridges of forested dune plummet down to swampy depressions and rare freshwater ponds. Oaks, hickories, beech trees and even towering magnolias form a canopy overhead that seems to mask what century you're in. It's easy to forget that you're on a sand island with breaking ocean waves and all the trappings of a resort town nearby.

Radford Tillett of Kitty Hawk is believed to be the last living person to have memories of the Nags Head Woods community. He visited his grandparents Maggie and Erb Tillett in the Woods as a child and remembers it fondly: "There weren't a lot of people to talk to, you just had family and friends. It was just a quieter time, it was just an easier time to live, I thought. It was a good time to be down here."[89]

Nellie was born Nellie Myrtle Midgett in 1918 to Mattie and Jethro Midgett, and her roots on the Outer Banks ran deep. Her kinfolk were farmers, fishermen, lifesavers, shipwreck salvagers and entrepreneurs of an authentic Outer Banks stripe. Toward the south end of the Woods community is where Nellie Myrtle's grandparents William Otis Twiford and Penelope Russell Twiford built their home after they were married in 1890. In a hand-drawn map of former Nags Head Woods homesteads by resident Ester Beacham, number 18 is labeled "Bill and Nellie Twiford."[90] In addition to being Nellie Myrtle's namesake, her grandmother Nellie Twiford was the postmistress and Bill served in the U.S. Lifesaving Service at both the Nags Head and Kill Devil Hills stations. The couple cared for their homestead and raised a family on their 16.7-acre parcel in the Woods. They also amassed a considerable tract of land that stretched from ocean to sound, known as the Twiford Tract. The 772.26 acres included the area where Wilbur and Orville Wright had successfully flown the world's first airplane in 1903.[91]

The Twifords' daughter, Mattie, married fisherman Jethro Midgett, and together they built and opened her general store in 1914, when she was just

A young Jethro and Mattie Midgett, Nellie Myrtle's father and mother. Mattie opened her general store on the soundside at the age of seventeen, and it became a hub of the community. *Photo courtesy of the Nellie Myrtle Pridgen Beachcomber Collection.*

seventeen. A community hub, "Miss Mattie's" was located on their one-hundred-by-one-hundred-foot lot on the Nags Head soundside, in the same area where Malachi Russell (a relation) had opened the first hotel in Nags Head in the 1800s.[92] Nellie could claim an industrious lineage indeed. Her people, hardworking and resourceful, lived on the Outer Banks at a time when not many others considered it their permanent residence. Bankers raised livestock, fished the waters and leaned on their network of family and neighbors to get by.

While the residents living here for generations were protected by the woods, they were not unconnected from the outside world. Skiffs and sailboats easily carried Bankers across the sound to the town of Manteo and the village of Wanchese on Roanoke Island, as well as to other Outer Banks communities where they had family, friends and business. By the 1850s, steamboats from Edenton, Hertford and Elizabeth City traveled by river and across the sounds to bring news, freight and passengers to the Outer Banks. Until the mid-1930s, the steamboat *Trenton* made runs between Elizabeth City, Nags Head and Manteo six days a week. Locals enjoyed daily mail service and often hitched rides on the mail boat.[93]

OLD NAGS HEAD AND THE "SUMMER PEOPLE"

The soundside was the only area where people vacationed on the Outer Banks around the turn of the century, though several summer cottages had begun to pop up on the oceanfront. The soundside resort boasted two hotels, a pavilion and a ferry dock to receive visitors. Locals would join the out-of-towners and gather at the pavilion to socialize, dance and hear live music.[94]

The permanent residents quickly recognized that servicing the visitors was a lucrative business opportunity. Many loaded up carts that could travel across the sand and went house to house peddling fresh produce, seafood, meat and poultry to the vacationing families. Women and girls found employment as domestic workers, cleaning cottages and taking in washing. Nellie's early childhood involved catering to these "summer people" and helping her parents in their tourism trades.[95]

In the afternoons, Jethro would set up the day's haul in a square of nets forming a shallow-water pen near the wharf and hotels. Female tourists would point out the fish they wanted for their family's supper. It was the job of Nellie and her brother, Jethro Jr., to wrangle the wriggling fish with their hands. Nellie's daughter, Carmen Gray, has cited the task as a formative experience for her mother, one that would lead her to seek the solitude of nature and the escape of beachcombing in later years.

"Those summertime ladies stood up there [on the dock] in their bonnets and long dresses and told Nell what fish they wanted," she explained. "They'd point down and Nell would have to catch the fish with her hands." Carmen claimed that her mother viewed the job as an "indignity."[96] She didn't like being ordered around. She couldn't stand the slimy feel of the fish. "She hated the job, she hated the women, she hated her father," said Carmen bluntly.[97]

Even as a child, it would seem, Nell was offended by her home being used as a playground by the well-to-do and her family and neighbors pandering to them. Fiercely protective of the wild and unspoiled Nags Head that she knew, Nellie had even more disdain for the development that the 1920s and '30s ushered in. In her pivotal adolescent years, locals saw the tourism industry set its roots, spread east toward the oceanfront and blossom in ways that transformed the way of life on the Outer Banks.

Arrival of the Tourism Machine: The 1920s and '30s on the Outer Banks

The 1920s and '30s ushered in a series of legislation and infrastructure projects to make the area safer and more accessible to outsiders. Between 1928 and 1931, wooden bridges were erected across the Currituck and Roanoke Sounds. They effectively connected the barrier islands to the mainland, opening up automobile access to the Outer Banks for the first time. An eighteen-mile paved road running the length of the island from Kitty Hawk to Nags Head was completed by 1931. The sand and asphalt "beach road" allowed for the safe flow of automobile traffic (locals had been driving cars on narrow, sandy paths shared with horses and carts since the early 1900s).[98]

The Depression era's New Deal brought men over the bridges from the Civilian Conservation Corps and the U.S. Transient Services to complete a series of projects. They built over one hundred miles of dunes along the

The bridge connecting Roanoke Island to Nags Head (*seen in distance*) in 1950. Beginning in the 1920s, bridges began to connect the Outer Banks to surrounding areas for the first time. *Photo courtesy of the Outer Banks History Center.*

Mattie Midgett's former store on Highway 12 in Nags Head, 2007. Still standing today, it is listed on the National Register of Historic Places and once operated as the Outer Banks Beachcomber Museum, displaying Nellie Myrtle's remarkable collection. It is now a private residence, closed to the public. *Photo courtesy of the State Archives of North Carolina.*

oceanfront to protect it from beach erosion and overwash, then ran sand fencing and planted beach grass to help stabilize the new dunes. The state outlawed the open grazing of animals (a common practice on the Outer Banks) with the Livestock Act of 1935. The decade even saw the dedication of the Outer Banks' first man-made tourist attraction: the Wright Brothers National Memorial. All of these efforts were to facilitate and encourage the booming tourism industry that had been envisioned for the Dare Beaches.[99]

This transition to tourism came at a pivotal point in Nellie Myrtle's upbringing and would color the rest of her life. It shaped her into a strong character who would become a force to be reckoned with and remembered. She correctly realized the impact that opening up access to the isolated barrier islands would have decades down the road. The rest of the Midgett family sensed it, too. It was the shift to tourism that ultimately drew them out of the Woods and into the sand and sunlight of the oceanfront.

In 1933, when Nell was fifteen, the family relocated their grocery and the family home to the oceanside, rolling the structures due east atop timbers and resting them at milepost 13 on the beach road, where they still stand today. While it was originally thought that the home was built sometime after the store, old photos and documents belonging to the family revealed a different story. After being moved oceanside, the gently sagging, cedar-

The Twiford-Midgett house, pictured here in 2007. Originally built in Nags Head Woods circa 1890, it was presumably moved to the beach road in 1933, where it stands today, and has since undergone repairs. *Photo courtesy of the State Archives of North Carolina.*

shingled house began to give away clues to its true age and identity as it slowly weathered over the years. Old framing techniques and cuts of lumber became exposed, and it was determined that the house was most likely built between 1880 and 1910, predating the family's oral history by decades. Further investigation turned up old aerial photos, deeds and plat drawings, leading to the discovery that the house is likely the Twiford-Midgett home, built circa 1890, where Nellie Myrtle's grandparents raised their family. This makes it the last surviving home from the disappeared village in Nags Head Woods.[100]

The Midgett family witnessed a wave of tourism wash over the island. Business boomed, people rushed in, new hotels and restaurants popped up—all catering to tourists. The Outer Banks were a place of leisure, replete with fishing, boating, hunting, sunbathing and relaxing "away from civilization."

Then came World War II, effectively halting the tourism machine as Americans poured their time and resources into the war machine. German U-boats lingered offshore. Outer Bankers blacked out their windows at night. Along with her father and brother and droves of other locals, Nellie Myrtle commuted to nearby Norfolk, Virginia, each week to contribute to the war effort. She worked at the Naval Air Station as the only woman in a crew of hydraulic mechanics. She had been twice married and twice

Nellie Myrtle Pridgen worked as a hydraulic mechanic during World War II at the Naval Air Station in Norfolk, Virginia. She was the only woman on the crew. *Photo courtesy of the Nellie Myrtle Pridgen Beachcomber Collection.*

Nellie Myrtle Pridgen holds the neck of a bottle that she found washed ashore up to an issue of *National Geographic* depicting the same. She was an avid reader with a thirst for knowledge and a heart for history. *Photo courtesy of the Outer Banks History Center.*

separated by this time. If Nellie Myrtle had never married, she would have been remembered as a Midgett. Pridgen isn't well known as an Outer Banks name, and marriage didn't suit her anyway. It seems she could have dropped the name as easily as she did the man. Nellie was fiercely, authentically Outer Banks. Every weekend she left Norfolk and returned to her native Nags Head and her two children, Carmen and Elwood, who were looked after by Mattie while their mother was away. She returned to her stretch of beach, where she picked up debris from the war that washed ashore—coffee mugs from naval vessels, rations of jam and chocolate, military-issue flashlights—and added them to her collection before returning again to Norfolk.[101]

Postwar Nags Head and Nellie Myrtle's Protective Shell

After the war, tourism resumed, as did Nell's disdain, perhaps due to the fact that she had to turn to tourism full time to make a living. When her aging parents, Mattie and Jethro, moved from the house into the living space above the family's store, Nellie Myrtle took over managing the two-story cottage. Appropriately dubbing it "The Last Resort," she rented rooms (and even hammocks strung up on the covered porch) and provided breakfast for visitors, including musicians who came through town to play at the legendary Outer Banks Casino.[102] Nellie Myrtle was a regular attendee at town and county meetings to advocate for the environment and to voice her objections to further development, like the addition of the Bypass (U.S. Highway 158), which was completed in 1959.

Nell's beachcombing became ritualistic, bordering on obsessive. She walked the mile-long stretch of sand at dawn and dusk and, when she needed to, sought the solitude of the sea.

"Nell would go out and swim, and wouldn't come back for a long time," said Dorothy Hope, a close family friend. "She was a dot like the head of a pin out there. That was her peace."[103]

Hope purchased the property from the family in 2002 and has been its caretaker along with her partner, Chaz Winkler, since. They worked to get it listed on the National Register of Historic Places and operated it intermittently as the Outer Banks Beachcomber Museum, with Nell's beachcombing collection displayed on the shelves of the old grocery that once held sacks of flour, jars of preserves and other staples. For years they

A six-piece band plays at the Nags Head Casino in 1950. Nellie Myrtle offered musicians room and board in the family's former home after turning it into a bed-and-breakfast she called "The Last Resort." *Photo courtesy of the Outer Banks History Center.*

acted as stewards of the property and its history and worked to establish it as a local heritage attraction.

On a blustery March day, in the office and former museum entrance, Hope motions through a doorway in her home into the section of the building that was once Mattie's store.

"There's a plastic bag in there and it's got part of a brick in it that says 'This is the brick that broke the windshield out of the Buick.'" She laughs, then drops her voice and adds more sternly, "You did not mess with Nell."[104]

Trespassers learned the hard way. In another fabled vehicle vandalization, Nell spray-painted the windshield of some casino patrons who had made the mistake of parking out in front of her property. In the mid-70s, after her parents had passed away, she moved into their former accommodations above the store. She dragged her collection of sea-tumbled bricks out from under the house and into the driveway, forming a physical barrier as she herself grew more reclusive and intolerant of outsiders.[105]

A portion of Nellie Myrtle Pridgen's prolific beachcombing collection displayed on the shelves of her mother's old general store, 2007. *Photo courtesy of the State Archives of North Carolina.*

In 1987, *National Geographic* reporter Charles E. Cobb Jr. found the front of her home barricaded with cinder blocks and wooden planks, along with a hand-painted sign warning in red letters to "Keep Out!" But Nell did have a soft side. She granted Cobb an interview. A reporter in her own right, she had amassed her own library of magazine and newspaper clippings pertaining to the Outer Banks and its environment and never hesitated to call up the local paper with story corrections and a demand for a reprint or retraction. She positioned herself as the expert and showed Cobb her beachcombing collection as proof. She even invited him to walk her stretch of beach. When he asked "what she thought of the development pressing in all around her along an asphalt strip she remembered as beach," she brusquely replied, "Some call it progress, I call it rape."[106]

"She Had No Idols Except the Ocean"

Today, the Outer Banks continues to break its own tourism records nearly every year. In 2020, despite being closed to visitors for two months at the outset of the COVID-19 pandemic, Dare County alone brought in $1.9 billion in tourism revenue. The Cape Hatteras National Seashore logged

A group of bathers at Nags Head circa the 1940s. Visitors began to migrate from the soundside to the oceanside as the Outer Banks tourism industry rapidly expanded in the 1930s, facilitated by infrastructure projects like a paved "beach road," completed in 1931. *Photo courtesy of the Nellie Myrtle Pridgen Beachcomber Collection.*

2.5 million visitors to the area and then broke that record the following year in 2021.[107] With the seasonal influx of people and business comes noisy traffic, merrymaking, restaurants full to capacity and a power grid working overtime. But there was a time when the wind whistling across flat expanses of sand, the screeching of gulls and the roaring of ocean waves provided the soundtrack to the Outer Banks. These are the sounds Nellie Myrtle heard on her walks as she combed the beach, even as development branched out all around her.

Nellie Myrtle Pridgen left behind a legacy in her renowned beachcomber collection. The discerning eyes and hands of the Outer Banks native preserved generations of artifacts washed ashore: the secrets of the sea given up only to her. As her late daughter Carmen Gray once said, "She had no idols, except the ocean." Though she grew increasingly solitary and bitter in her later years, it was in part because she cared so much. "She had a rough exterior, but that was not the true Nell," said Carmen. "It was a facade; she was a very kind, dear person."[108]

In a way, she was in mourning for a place that was shifting and slipping away from her, like the sand beneath her feet. Her grief manifested in a beachcombing habit that left us all with the priceless gift of her collection—our history preserved.

On a stormy September day in 1992, guests gathered by invitation only on Nell's stretch of beach to celebrate her life. She had passed away in July, in the height of tourist season, but her loved ones knew better than to schedule

Nellie Myrtle in her element. She combed this stretch of beach in Nags Head across seven decades, collecting countless treasures spit from the sea. *Photo courtesy of the Nellie Myrtle Pridgen Beachcomber Collection.*

the service then. To honor her, they waited until after Labor Day, when the Outer Banks again grew quiet. Nell's son-in-law Billy Gray and family friend Eddie Reber Jr. set out in a dory with her ashes. As Dorothy Hope gazes out from Nell's former home, across the street and seaward, she remembers it:

> *I thought that boat was going to flip, but they got out there. Billy put those ashes in the water and the dolphin came up right as they went in and just rode right alongside them. And the pelicans came down, and the wind came up and it was time to go back inside. It was fitting for her. I feel I look out there and I can see her…She was a force to be reckoned with, I tell you.*[109]

Chapter 5

SAVING OUR SAND DUNES

Carolista Baum, 1970s

From these hearts shall burst new energy
And new generations of women will plot to save sand dunes
And dream of being governor
And create new designs in gold upon the sand.
—from "Carolista," by Claustin Jenkins

She Shall Not Be Moved: Carolista Stands Down a Bulldozer

The Baum children left their family cottage on the oceanfront in Nags Head and set out westward across the sand. After a safe escort across the beach road and the two-lane bypass, they were free to take off alone up the golden face of Jockey's Ridge, the East Coast's tallest living sand dune. Exploring its ridges and pools, its wind-battered edges and quiet forested areas, they played until it was time to return home at day's end. So it went for many sandy summer days.

Until one morning in 1973, when the three siblings heard an unusual sound. It drowned out the familiar call of seabirds and rhythmic lapping of waves in their Neverland. They discovered that the droning noise belonged to a bulldozer, poised to dig into the sand near the base of the dune. The eldest of the Baum children, Ann-Cabell, led her sister and brother, Inglis and Gibbs, back to the one person who they knew could right the wrong: their mother, Carolista Baum.

A smiling Carolista Baum with the wind in her hair on Jockey's Ridge, 1989. *Photo courtesy of the Outer Banks History Center.*

Hearing the news, their neighbors all along Cottage Row felt defeated as they realized that development had found its way to Jockey's Ridge. Ann-Cabell launched an accusation at the adults: "You're just like everyone else—all talk and doing nothing!"[110] With that, Carolista walked across to the dunes to find the bulldozer and planted herself firmly in front of it in the sand. She informed the machine's operator that she would not move from the spot until he shut it down. It worked. Disarmed by her genteel disposition and commanding presence, he climbed down and left the jobsite for the day. Carolista was quick to take the machine's distributor cap to ensure its continued immobility while she planned her next move.

"THE GRANDADDY DUNE": GEOLOGY OF JOCKEY'S RIDGE

The sand dune system of Jockey's Ridge formed an estimated three thousand to four thousand years ago when strong storms and hurricanes pushed massive amounts of sand onto the beach from large offshore shoals. However, dunes of this size don't occur anywhere else along the string of barrier islands that makes up North Carolina's Outer Banks. Jockey's Ridge is uniquely positioned on a stretch of land where prevailing winds and seasonal storms act in direct opposition to one another. Strong storms known as nor'easters and counterclockwise-spinning hurricanes dredge up and deposit sand as they batter the land from the northeast. Then prevailing southwesterly winds push the sand back toward the beach from the exact opposite direction.[111] Like an outspread deck of cards being turned over and back again by the hand of a magician, the sand is continually moved back and forth, keeping it from ever being blown away entirely.

Jockey's Ridge looms large over homes along Soundside Road in Nags Head. It is the tallest living sand dune on the East Coast. *Photo courtesy of the Outer Banks History Center.*

The constantly shifting dune can reach heights of sixty up to one hundred feet and was used by early European explorers as a navigational landmark seen from sea. In the mid-1800s, the first hotels popped up at the base of the dune along the soundside to accommodate wealthy planter and merchant families seeking sea breezes as they escaped from the stifling heat of their inland plantations and farms. A wharf, an entertainment pavilion and a general store soon followed, and the early seeds of tourism on the Outer Banks were sown there in the sand. But the behemoth dune soon pushed into hotel rooms and inched toward the rooflines of the cluster of buildings, prompting their owners to relocate them or surrender them to the sand.[112]

Carolista's family can also trace a long history in eastern North Carolina. A native of Edenton, North Carolina, Carolista's grandmother was the famed historical novelist Inglis Fletcher. The Baums split their time between Chapel Hill and Nags Head, where they spent summers in their oceanfront cottage built in 1905. Over the course of the twentieth century, it stood in line with a few dozen others along historic Cottage Row, but nothing much surrounded them except vast stretches of sand. A few homes still dotted the soundside on the back side of Jockey's Ridge, but that area was

Visitors prepare to walk up Jockey's Ridge in 1989. It officially became a state park in 1975, due in large part to Carolista Baum's tireless efforts. *Photo courtesy of the Outer Banks History Center.*

no longer a thoroughfare or as much of a destination for visitors as it had been at the turn of the century. In the 1930s, tourism's focus shifted from the soundside to the oceanfront. What drew people to the stretch of the Outer Banks where the Baums spent their time was the giant sand hill. The Baum children were friendly to visitors when they encountered them climbing their sandy playground in wonderment, but they knew that the presence of the bulldozer meant something else entirely. It was discovered that sections of the dune were slated to be flattened and developed as a residential community. When the earthmover powered down for the day, it was a victory for the audacious Carolista and her allies, but she knew the fight for Jockey's Ridge was just beginning.

SOS: SAVE OUR SAND DUNES

"What a pity that beach cottages and other buildings, no matter how attractive in their own right, should nestle right up against Jockey's Ridge and mar in a matter of months what nature had constructed over a course of centuries," read an article in the June 1975 issue of *We the People of*

North Carolina. It was a sentiment shared by many locals and visitors alike. Though there had been talk of preserving the dunes for some time, no concrete action had yet been taken. In fact, it was generally assumed that such a natural wonder already had some form of protection or designation, but this was not the case. The land was privately owned. Developer and businessman Percy Meekins owned the parcel that was being threatened, but after confronting Carolista, he agreed to hold off on his project. Carolista and her first husband, Walter Baum, promptly penned a petition to the State of North Carolina entitled "Save Our Sand Dunes," and it garnered twenty-five thousand signatures in the first week.[113]

What followed was a comprehensive, ambitious and creative campaign designed and spearheaded by Carolista and carried out by the People to Preserve Jockey's Ridge, the nonprofit she had formed. She launched a community effort to educate and rally the public around the cause. Schoolchildren collected loose change in cardboard canisters and sold square

A promotional poster depicting Jockey's Ridge for Carolista Baum's Save Our Sand Dunes campaign, 1974. *Photo courtesy of the Outer Banks History Center.*

feet of the dune to donors for five dollars (for which they received a handsome certificate in the mail). The group peddled bumper stickers, T-shirts, kites and all grades of merchandise. Readers of the local newspaper could write in for their Jockey's Ridge paraphernalia "featuring 'the grandaddy dune,'" which included bumper stickers, notepads, placemats, kites, a fifteen-minute documentary film on the area and even a limited-edition silkscreen that Carolista herself designed.[114]

Carolista had her own children man a bright pink wooden hut that she had moved near the dunes, where they sold Save Our Sand Dunes merchandise and collected donations.[115] The adults appealed to local government, state officials, prominent citizens and the owners of the acreage making up Jockey's Ridge. Carolista handled the big names herself. For three days, she sat patiently in the office of North Carolina governor James Hunt until he agreed to speak with her.[116] Along with her persistence, Carolista's most effective tool was her charisma. She was charming and beautiful, known for her generous spirit and a smile like sunshine.

CAROLISTA'S COTTAGES: PRESERVING THE ORIGINAL OUTER BANKS

To manage the many operations of the People to Preserve Jockey's Ridge, a headquarters was set up in Carolista's jewelry shop. Aside from her demonstrated expertise as a conservationist, lobbyist, marketing maven, organizer and influencer, Carolista was a jewelry designer and artist by trade. In 1962, she opened her first studio on the Outer Banks in a tiny structure that once served as the icehouse for the Nags Head Hotel on the soundside. Her welcoming nature and beautiful pieces of wearable art drew a devoted clientele, and in 1966 she relocated her jewelry studio to a larger building. Named "Carolista's," it was advertised as the first jewelry store on the Outer Banks and was known for its distinctive round second story.[117]

With a proclivity to preserve, Carolista created her own unique cottage court behind her shop out of salvaged structures. As historic Nags Head hotels and cottages were slated for demolition, Carolista and her husband would often purchase their outbuildings and move them to their property, where she would renovate them to rent to tourists, seasonal employees and year-round residents. The small village she created was like a living history exhibit of the area. The compound included the old parsonage from St. Andrew's Episcopal Church, built in 1868; the detached garage from the

Left: Carolista Baum's jewelry studio in Nags Head, 1967. In later years, it became known by partygoers as the Round House. *Photo courtesy of the Outer Banks History Center, Aycock Brown Collection.*

Below: Carolista Baum and her first husband, Walter Baum, at work in their Nags Head jewelry studio, 1967. *Photo courtesy of the Outer Banks History Center, Aycock Brown Collection.*

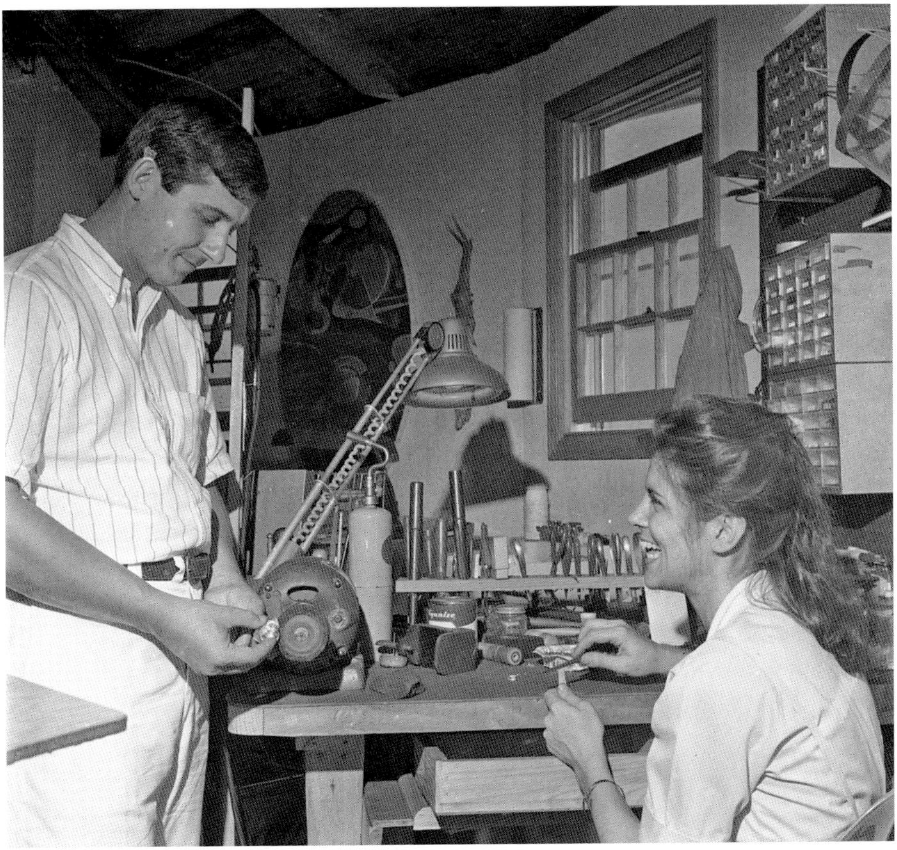

First Colony Inn, built in 1932; and an outbuilding of the Arlington Hotel, a turn-of-the-century establishment built on the soundside and later relocated to the oceanfront.[118] The landmark hotel was washed into the ocean after a heavy storm in 1973, but thanks to Carolista's appreciation for history, a small part of it remained in her village of historic cottages for many years, becoming known as "the Party House." In later years, her jewelry studio would come to be known as a popular party house in its own right, known by locals as "the Round House."

Jockey's Ridge Jamboree: The Dune Receives State Park Status

With her sights set on a goal, Carolista was unstoppable. While keeping her business running in the jewelry shop, she employed her children as secretaries for the People to Preserve Jockey's Ridge, having them dial and redial numbers on the rotary phone until she got the answers she was looking for. When Ann-Cabell came down with pneumonia, she relocated the operation to the family cottage and kept the phone calls going.[119] When Carolista severed a finger while making jewelry, she taught herself to write and work with her left hand. During the off-season and winter months, she moved the Save Our Sand Dunes campaign headquarters to her shop in Chapel Hill, farther from her beloved dunes but conveniently closer to state legislative offices. A mere few months after Carolista stood down the bulldozer, the People to Preserve Jockey's Ridge group was successful in lobbying the state Division of Parks and Recreation to complete a feasibility study on making the dunes into a state park, of which they were in favor.[120]

The next victory came in 1974, when Jockey's Ridge was declared a Natural National Landmark. Although this designation didn't guarantee the land's protection, it did help bolster the campaign's efforts.

The following year, their efforts paid off when the 1975 General Assembly appropriated $500,000 to acquire land for the creation of Jockey's Ridge State Park. Along with the use of matching federal funds, the State of North Carolina bought 152 acres of Jockey's Ridge from Percy Meekins and several other Nags Head families who were in favor of the preservation efforts themselves. The Nature Conservancy bought another large tract, including the adjacent Nags Head Woods.[121] The remaining land was purchased with funds raised by the People to Preserve Jockey's Ridge—by the hands and hearts of devoted Outer Bankers and visitors.

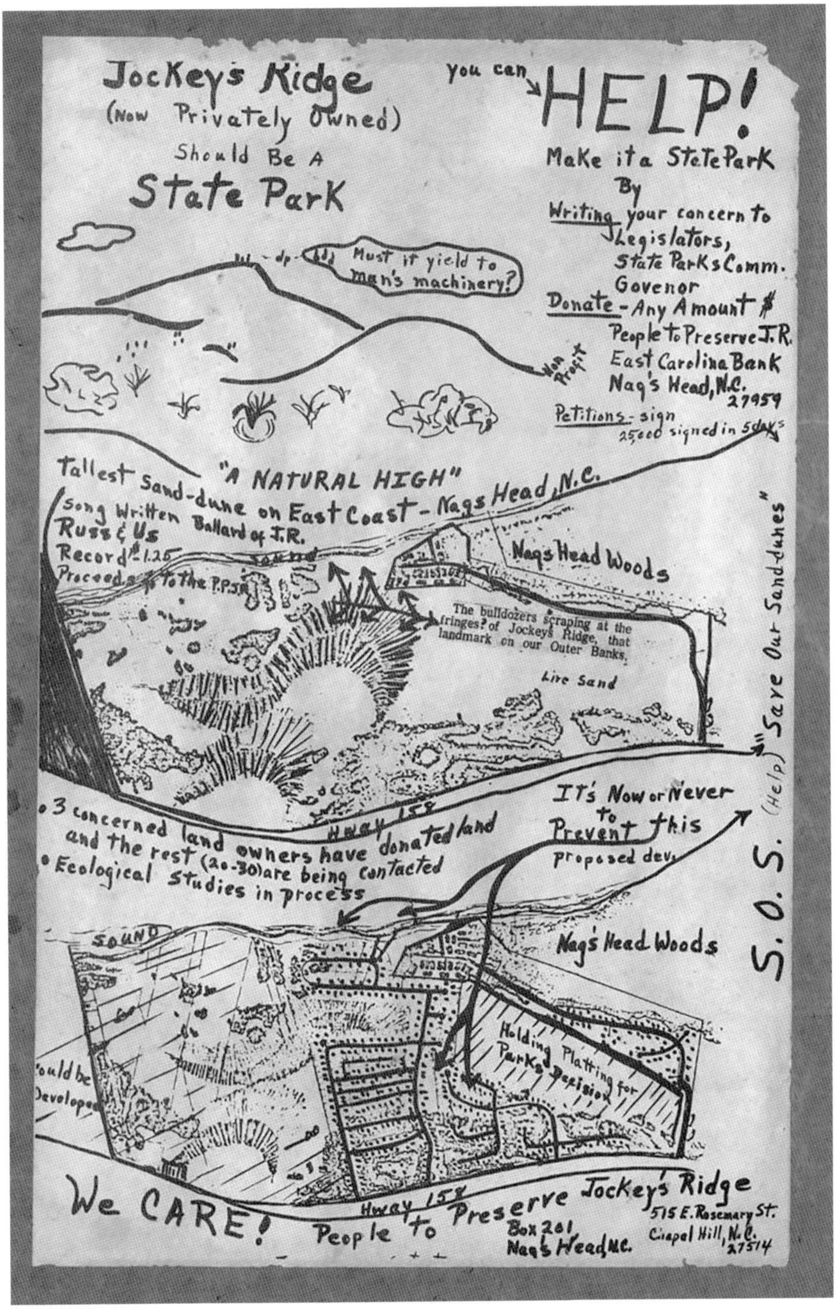

This hand-drawn poster from the People to Preserve Jockey's Ridge includes a map of the proposed residential development and urges the public's help in making the natural area into a state park. *Photo courtesy of the Outer Banks History Center.*

A poster for the Jockey's Ridge Jamboree, a weekend-long event to celebrate the dunes being recognized as a Natural National Landmark and to raise awareness for the action still needed in order for them to become a state park. *Photo courtesy of the Outer Banks History Center.*

Park Ranger Fran Crutchfield explains how fulgurite is created when lightning strikes sand, 1991. The designation of Jockey's Ridge as a state park opened up jobs and educational opportunities for locals and visitors alike. *Photo courtesy of the Outer Banks History Center.*

In a 1976 film titled *Jockey's Ridge for All the People*, Carolista is shown on the dunes, wearing her signature knowing smile as she waits beside a podium. Her dark hair is piled atop her head in the elegant windswept updo so often seen in photographs of the conservationist. It is May 31, 1975, and the audience is barefoot in the sand, sporting shaggy hair and flared pants in classic seventies style. They are gathered for the Jockey's Ridge Jamboree, a dedication ceremony celebrating the first tract of land purchased by the People to Preserve Jockey's Ridge as it was officially handed over to the State of North Carolina.

David Stick, famed local author and historian, introduces Carolista, and she takes the stage. In an elegant, commanding southern drawl, she begins by humbly acknowledging that "there are thousands of people that are not here today that are also responsible." She hands over the deed for the tract of land to the director of state parks, Tom Ellis. It was purchased with "nickels, dimes, and quarters raised by the public school children and by five dollar donations for square feet," she announces.[122] Though she never wanted to take full credit, Jockey's Ridge State Park was established in 1975 due in large part to the unwavering dedication, energy and brilliance of Carolista Baum.

PATRON SAINT OF PRESERVATION ON THE OUTER BANKS: THE LEGACY OF CAROLISTA BAUM

Having won their fight, the People to Preserve Jockey's Ridge disbanded in the late seventies. But the unstoppable Carolista wasn't finished saving the Outer Banks just yet. She became the president of the Chicamacomico Historical Association, fighting to preserve the Chicamacomico Lifesaving Station, famous for the legendary *Mirlo* rescue but abandoned by the U.S. Coast Guard in 1954.[123] She received a North Carolina Historic Preservation Award of Merit in 1977 for her role in saving the station, just two years after saving the dunes.[124] She also served as the chairperson of the U.S.S. Monitor Research Council, advocating for the shipwreck that was discovered in 1973. Due in part to her efforts, it was named as the first-ever national marine sanctuary in 1975.[125]

After making the move to the Outer Banks full time, Carolista spent her remaining years raising her children, taking in tenants and enjoying her work and her family on the sandy barrier islands to which she was so devoted. After a short but full life, Carolista Fletcher Baum Golden passed

Above: Park Ranger George Barnes presents a plaque to Peggy Birkemeier and the Junior Friends of Jockey's Ridge in 1991. The group continued Carolista's legacy by advocating for the creation of a visitor's center and nature trails at the park after her passing. *Photo courtesy of the Outer Banks History Center.*

Opposite: Carolista Baum seated at Jockey's Ridge. Her indomitable spirit and hard work led to it becoming a state park rather than a condominium complex. She is credited with preserving the tallest living dune system in the eastern United States for future generations. *Photo courtesy of the Outer Banks History Center.*

away in 1991. Memories of the beloved, vivacious Nags Header are colored by descriptions of her radiant smile, her charm, her grace and the love she exuded for her family and friends. She never knew a stranger and she never backed down from what she knew to be the right thing to do. She led a life that continues to inspire.

Picking up where Carolista left off, another nature lover named Peggy Birkemeier formed the Friends of Jockey's Ridge in the early nineties, which conducted research on the ridge, raised money to build a boardwalk for handicap access, lobbied for a visitor's center and established nature trails.[126] The road leading to the park's main entrance from the highway was named Carolista Drive in her honor. Today, Jockey's Ridge is the most visited state park in North Carolina. More than that, it is the legacy of Carolista Baum, left for all the people.

As the sun sets in the west at the close of each day on the Outer Banks, shadows reach seaward across the sand. The first is cast by Carolista's cottage at the edge of the foamy wash, the next by the remaining cluster of homes where her shop once stood between sea and sound. At last, the sun dips behind the ridge of the tallest living sand dune on the East Coast, and the land is enveloped in shadow. The warmth radiating from its golden sand, the memory of her smile, lingers still.

Chapter 6

MOVING A LIGHTHOUSE

Cheryl Shelton-Roberts, 1990s

Hatteras sits on the edge of the continent marking the line between sand and water, safety and danger. This light station site has witnessed all that has come to pass since the birth of this nation until the present. Its history is our history.
—Cheryl-Shelton Roberts in *Cape Hatteras: America's Lighthouse*

The senator was apologetic. His voice on the other end of the line was measured as he told Cheryl Shelton-Roberts, author, historian and cofounder of the Outer Banks Lighthouse Society, that he could no longer support the move of the Cape Hatteras Lighthouse. It was the late 1990s. After decades of controversy surrounding the fate of the iconic light, the best chance at saving it seemed to be slipping away.

The Nation's Tallest Brick Lighthouse

Completed in 1870, the Cape Hatteras Lighthouse measures 198 feet from the base of its foundation to the tip of the lightning rod on its tower, making it the tallest brick lighthouse in the United States, with 269 steps spiraling to its lantern room at the top. Over one million bricks were ordered for its construction, which took three years to complete. At its inaugural lighting, the lighthouse sat 1,500 feet from the shore and cast its beacon of light for sixteen miles.[127] It swept the surrounding area and illuminated the "Graveyard of the Atlantic," a grim name for the stretch of North Carolina's coastline along the Outer Banks plagued by treacherous shoals and thousands of shipwrecks. It even claimed the lives of several members of John White's company on his return voyage to Roanoke Island to search for the "lost colonists" in 1590. After safely crossing the ocean from England, seven men were lost to the sea while attempting to come ashore on the barrier islands. According to John White's written account of the voyage:

> *At this time the wind blew at northeast and direct into the harbor so great a gale, that the sea broke extremely on the* [sand] *bar, and the tide went very forcibly at the entrance....Captain Spicer came to the entrance of the breach with his mast standing up, and...a very dangerous sea broke into their boat and overset them quite, the men kept the boat some in it, and some hanging on it, but the next sea set the boat on ground, where it beat so, that some of them were forced to let go their hold, hoping to wade ashore; but the sea still beat them down, so that they could neither stand nor swim, and the boat twice or thrice was turned the keel upward, whereon Captain Spicer and Skinner hung until they sunk, & were seen no more.*[128]

The Cape Hatteras Lighthouse became a symbol of hope and safety to those traveling the dark and perilous strand of remote barrier islands. It provided stable, well-paying jobs to the islanders that held the honored position of keeper. It improved navigation and saved countless lives along the Eastern Seaboard. But after a century of enduring battering storms and worsening coastal erosion, its fall into the Atlantic seemed inevitable.

Beginning in the 1960s and carrying through to the end of the millennium, numerous academic studies assessed the state of the lighthouse. The science concluded again and again that it would indeed be lost to the encroaching Atlantic if no action was taken. By 1975, the tower was just 175 feet from the ocean. After a significant structural crack was found, it was closed to the public for repairs. By 1985, further beach erosion put just fifty to seventy feet of sand between the lighthouse and the pounding surf. After a piece of metal window trim weighing roughly forty pounds plummeted to the ground, the lighthouse was again closed to the public until 1993.[129]

It was clear that the Cape Hatteras Lighthouse, with its famous black-and-white diagonally striped daymark, was in danger and becoming dangerous to others. Orrin Pilkey, a marine geologist at Duke University, controversially suggested to "let it fall in" after publishing an academic article on the subject

In 1999, the Cape Hatteras Lighthouse stood only 120 feet from the shoreline. The beach had eroded dramatically since the lighthouse was erected in 1870, 1,500 feet from shore. *Photo courtesy of the Outer Banks History Center, Mike Booher Collection.*

in 1974. He concluded that "it is difficult but necessary to come to grips with the ultimate result of living with nature at the shoreline" and that "nothing is so important that it can't fall into the sea."[130]

The locals vehemently disagreed. To the people of Hatteras Island, many of whom could trace their lineage back to the first inhabitants of the Outer Banks, the lighthouse *was* that important. Many were descendants of lighthouse keepers. Generations of local families had watched its light sweep across the island, rhythmically peering into their bedroom windows as they were lulled to sleep each night. They used it as a fixed point to orient themselves on an ever-changing island. The idea of losing their true north was not something they could live with. Instead, they fought fiercely to protect it.

Extensive measures were taken by various government agencies to fortify the lighthouse's foundation and its surroundings, including beach nourishment, a process in which tons of sand are dredged from farther out in the ocean and pumped onto shore. Sandbags were used to barricade the foundation; three groins were built, and a seawall was proposed. There was even an attempt at an experimental technique that involved placing artificial sea grass along the shoreline to slow erosion. It proved ineffective.

The Dare County Library bookmobile, pictured here in front of the Cape Hatteras Lighthouse circa 1950, brought books to remote areas of the Outer Banks. *Photo courtesy of the State Library of North Carolina.*

Interest grew at the state and national level, and in 1981, U.S. senator Jesse Helms, Governor James Hunt of North Carolina and others formed the "Save the Lighthouse" committee.[131] The group gained influence as other prominent North Carolinians joined, like photographer and conservationist Hugh Morton, who had inherited and developed Grandfather Mountain. The group had powerful political sway and a mission that locals and the general public could rally behind. But in addition to being costly, all of their proposed measures to "save the lighthouse" were only temporary. Solid structures, like groins and sea walls, have proven to be counterproductive, causing further coastal erosion down the line.

AN UNPOPULAR IDEA

Then came a new idea. If the lighthouse couldn't be protected where it stood, the only hope for its survival was to move it out of harm's way. Though the two-hundred-foot brick tower weighed almost five thousand tons, engineers said that it could be done. The idea had actually been considered in the early 1980s but tossed out as impractical, if not impossible. Since that time, the engineering and technology involved in moving structures had advanced, bringing the idea back into the realm of possibility. The movement to move the lighthouse gained speed, with science on its side.

A 1988 report by the National Academy of Sciences recommended the relocation of the lighthouse after considering ten different options for protecting it. The report determined that moving the lighthouse would

Cheryl and her husband, Bruce Roberts, at the Cape Lookout Lighthouse near the Shackleford Banks. Together they cofounded the Outer Banks Lighthouse Society. *Photo courtesy of Cheryl-Shelton Roberts.*

actually be the most cost-effective tactic that could be employed to save it, and the National Park Service agreed, officially recommending relocation in 1989. North Carolina State University issued a report in 1997 reviewing and endorsing the National Academy of Science's conclusions from nearly a decade prior and urging that "the National Park Service proceed as soon as possible with its present plans to obtain the financial resources necessary to preserve the lighthouse by moving it."[132]

The research consistently determined that the risk of leaving the lighthouse where it was outweighed the risk of moving it. Nonetheless, those in favor of moving the lighthouse were met with fierce opposition to the idea of relocating a cultural heritage icon on Hatteras Island and found themselves butting heads with the popular "Save the Lighthouse" group, which proclaimed that moving the lighthouse in retreat from the shoreline would be "ceding man's historic battle against nature."[133] An overwhelming majority of locals agreed, fearing that the lighthouse would be damaged in the move. They also worried that it would lose its historical value and cultural significance in a new location. Some were so hurt by the idea of moving the light that they said they would rather gaze upon it as a pile of bricks lying in the surf than standing in a new location. In short, the idea broke their hearts. But one local couple that had recently moved to the area sided firmly with the idea of moving the lighthouse. Cheryl Shelton-Roberts and her husband, Bruce Roberts, understood the necessity—and the urgency—of moving the structure in order to save it.

For Love and Lighthouses: Cheryl and Bruce Make Advocacy a Team Effort

Cheryl met Bruce in 1991 after being widowed two years prior. He was the senior travel photographer at *Southern Living* magazine, where he had previously been the director of photography for the publication. The focus of his work was to capture stories of the American South, but his passion was for lighthouses. Cheryl's father also had a love of lighthouses, and her family took frequent trips to the coast from their home near Greensboro, North Carolina, growing up. Cheryl's mother told her that she was only six months old the first time she was taken to the top of the Cape Hatteras light. Cheryl spent twenty years as a classroom teacher, and when Bruce discovered that she was also a gifted writer, he welcomed her involvement in his projects. They traveled the Northeast and Great Lakes together,

Above: Cheryl Shelton-Roberts and John Gaskill at the Bodie Island Lighthouse circa 2010. John was the son of Lloyd Vernon Gaskill, the last keeper of the Bodie Island light. *Photo courtesy of Cheryl-Shelton Roberts.*

Opposite: Cheryl Shelton-Roberts touches the tip of the lightning rod at the top of the Bodie Island Lighthouse. This light station underwent restoration in 2008 and was opened to public climbing for the first time in 2013. *Photo courtesy of Cheryl-Shelton Roberts.*

researching and chronicling the lighthouses of those regions and having a "tremendous adventure."[134]

Together Cheryl and Bruce cofounded the Outer Banks Lighthouse Society in 1994, while living in Nags Head. Their initial focus was the Bodie Island Lighthouse on Pea Island, north of Cape Hatteras. The beautiful light station wrapped in horizontal black-and-white stripes was an important piece of Outer Banks history but was seemingly neglected and in need of restoration. They weren't aware that the Cape Hatteras light was in need of more immediate attention. When the couple took a trip down to Hatteras, "we thought we were going to see a lighthouse that had been moved," said Cheryl, explaining that money had been earmarked for it back in 1988. "Nothing had happened, and no one knew anything. They couldn't tell us anything." The two lighthouse historians now had two major projects on their plates, advocating for both the Bodie Island and Cape Hatteras Lighthouses. Their vision and goals for the Outer Banks Lighthouse Society began to crystalize. Today, the group works closely with the National Park Service and other government agencies and nonprofit groups to "achieve the safekeeping of the buildings, artifacts, and records of the United States Lighthouse Service," according to its website.

In 1997, Cheryl and Bruce coauthored their first book together, called *Lighthouse Families*. It included oral histories, historic photographs and even personal family recipes from lighthouse keepers and their kin all over the nation. Since then, they have coauthored over ten other books on lighthouses together, as well as numerous solo projects, publications and articles each. They were awarded the prestigious Holland Award in 2020, and Cheryl is also a recipient of the "Keeper of the Light" award from the American Lighthouse Foundation. She was editor of the Outer Banks Lighthouse Society's award-winning newsletter for twenty-six years.

As the debate over the fate of the Cape Hatteras Lighthouse was coming to a boil around 1997, Cheryl and Bruce were working on two book projects, including *Cape Hatteras: America's Lighthouse*, actively studying the light's history and interviewing scientists and engineers on its construction. They knew the Cape Hatteras light as a physical structure better than most. They also knew that the perspectives of the scientific, environmental and lighthouse groups with which they were involved were not shared by everyone. Cheryl recalls her opportunity to go up against Hugh Morton with a piece in the *News & Observer*:

> *At that time I was still very nervous and I never did come right out and directly say to move the lighthouse. I just said "the science is there, we need to make the right choice." I read that a little bit later and I thought, you chicken. You know, I was intimidated by a man. You've got to stand up and say what you know and what you feel is right. So in a way that was a turning point for me. That was around 1997 into 1998 where I really started the push forward.*[135]

One side would have to win over Congress and the National Park Service, which would ultimately decide the lighthouse's fate. Bitter disagreements, political alliances and even legal battles muddied the waters, making it difficult to secure funding for the move. After decades of turmoil and many players involved in the question of what to do with the beloved historic structure, one phone call would help to tip the scales.

THE ACHILLES' HEEL OF THE CAPE HATTERAS LIGHTHOUSE

Though more than twenty years have passed, Cheryl remembers the morning of the phone call vividly. When Senator Basnight rang to inform her that he had to change his position, she wasted no time in asking, "Marc, do you know about the foundation of that lighthouse?"

"No, tell me about it," came his response.

She had his ear. Drawing from her roles as an author, historian and educator, she began to inform the highly respected North Carolina politician, beloved by his native Outer Banks, about the lighthouse's Achilles' heel.

Due to high groundwater levels on the Outer Banks, she explained, the lighthouse's foundation had to be creatively engineered. Any hole dug deeper than four or five feet on these barrier islands will begin to fill with water, a problem the building crew immediately realized when it began work on the light in 1868. The superintendent of construction, Dexter Stetson, implemented an innovative "floating foundation" to get around this problem. Yellow pine timbers measuring six feet by twelve feet were laid in the foundation pit and submerged in a pool of fresh water. Granite plinths were then placed on top of the timbers, providing a rock-solid base to build upon. The design was effective, providing a solid foundation for more than a century. Likewise, it was a testament to the creative thinking and unconventional methods historically embraced by Outer Bankers inhabiting shifting stretches of sand. But with the shoreline eroding and the pounding surf moving closer to the base of the lighthouse with each passing year, the freshwater foundation was at risk of being inundated by salt water. If the freshwater pool was compromised, the salt water could degrade the pine timbers and eventually cause the structure to tip, if not collapse.[136]

Cheryl knew that aligning with the movement to move the lighthouse could be "political suicide" for Senator Basnight, "but he told the people that he would make the best decisions that he could and they knew that he always supported them. He did so much for the people of Dare County and they loved him, so his opinion was held in very high regard."

In the months leading up to the pivotal phone call, Cheryl found that the same was not true of her opinion. While caring for an aging mother, raising a young daughter, working on various publishing projects and "trying to live life normally," she reported "nasty notes" and even property damage by those seeking to intimidate her due to her stance on the lighthouse and the say she had in the matter. Her opponents even encouraged people to stay away from her business, Lighthouse Gallery & Gifts. The unrest became a factor in her family's decision to relocate.

"We decided to move a few ferry rides south to get away from all of the negativity," she said. "I wish we hadn't left, if I could go back, I would not leave." But her relocation was not a surrender. The Outer Banks Lighthouse Society became a public voice for the move, essentially acting as an unofficial PR group for the National Park Service. The group would write letters, publish pamphlets and provide pieces for local and regional media outlets, pushing out information for the cause.

"We could see the future, and we could see what needed to be done. We knew it was going to take some time and require some money. But there were a lot of emotions involved," said Cheryl.

Speaking from the Heart

This became apparent at an emotionally charged meeting held at the North Carolina Aquarium on Roanoke Island on April 9, 1998, which Cheryl points to as a significant event in the timeline of the lighthouse's move. The public meeting had been arranged by United States senator Lauch Faircloth and congressman Walter Jones to discuss the lighthouse and the erosion that threatened it. The local paper "strongly discouraged" any groups that were "non-lighthouse related" from attending, as space was limited, and urged them to stay home and listen to the live radio broadcast instead. On the afternoon of the meeting, roughly a dozen news crews were on hand, and the event drew a crowd of close to eight hundred people. Many carried signs and wore Save the Lighthouse T-shirts, strongly opposing the move.[137]

Cheryl was chosen as one of ten expert witnesses to speak at the meeting, based on "their expertise with coastal issues and with the lighthouse in particular."[138] The panel of experts, some in favor of moving the lighthouse and some opposed, would then be questioned by Senator Faircloth and Congressman Jones, followed by public comment and questioning. The meeting started off rocky; Cheryl recalls being aggressively pushed aside as she made her way into the meeting room, her aggressor barging his way in front of her to set foot through the door first. The tone for the event had been set.

Key players like Morton and Jones supported additional anti-erosion measures and pointed out things like the loss of the "dramatic photographic opportunity" of the lighthouse sitting on the edge of the sea if it was moved. Locals were roused by this and other sentimental appeals. On April 7, two days before the April 9 meeting at the aquarium on Roanoke Island, another meeting was held at the North Carolina Museum of History in Raleigh. The Save Cape Hatteras Lighthouse Committee held a press briefing with "documentation and expert testimony that the lighthouse can and must be maintained in place." Fearing that the lighthouse would be damaged or destroyed in the expensive "scheme" proposed by the

National Park Service, the group sought to prove that "the lighthouse can be protected safely in place for less than half the money requested by the Park Service."[139]

Back in Dare County, Cheryl sat in the crowd, preparing for her turn to speak. A representative for North Carolina governor James Hunt was set to speak before her. A few weeks earlier, Cheryl had been contacted by the representative's office and asked to send through a copy of her speech, so the two speeches would not be redundant. But as the governor's staffer took to the podium, speaking on his behalf, she began to deliver Cheryl's speech verbatim. Cheryl's stomach sank.

"She read my whole speech," Cheryl recalled. "She thought I had written that speech for her." She graciously chalked it up to a misunderstanding. But as she listened to her own carefully penned words being read to the crowd, she realized "I've got nothing." And she was up next.

She rose to make her way to the podium and saw her many opponents in the audience, some with arms crossed, some holding signs and posters against the move. She also saw friends and colleagues who had been working tirelessly in support of the move. She focused her eyes on her friend and current president of the Outer Banks Lighthouse Society, Bett Padgett, and spoke from her heart:

> *I know this is tough on a lot of people, but we are looking at an historic structure that is genuinely the strongest coastal icon in North America. For many years, immigrants coming to the United States saw the Statue of Liberty and, in many cases, the other first symbols of America that they saw were the lighthouses. Travel was by water and lighthouses were the backbone of the economy. It deserves to be saved if we have the power to save it.*

This is how, many years later, Cheryl summarized the speech she made that day.[140] She also shared success stories of other lighthouses that had been moved.[141] While speaking her truth to the packed house was a personal victory, Cheryl suspects the fervor of the April 9 meeting at the aquarium is what made Senator Basnight reverse course on his support of the idea to move the lighthouse. He was in attendance as well and led off the remarks by the ten expert witnesses, calling the decision over the lighthouse's fate "one of the most difficult issues I've ever dealt with." Though he had been largely supportive of the move, the *Coastland Times* reported that Basnight "walked the proverbial political fence" at the meeting, saying that he would support either side when a decision was reached.[142]

It was after the heated meeting that the senator called Cheryl to tell her that he could no longer support the move of the Cape Hatteras Lighthouse. Cheryl knew she could no longer afford to be timid or passive about her stance on the issue. Armed with information about the threat to the lighthouse's floating foundation, she spoke with him for over an hour and was able to convince him that moving the lighthouse was the only way to save it.

Not long after his phone call with Cheryl, Senator Basnight brought news that he had secured an appointment with President Clinton to discuss the fate of the Cape Hatteras light. He took a model of the highly recognizable lighthouse from the Roberts's gallery and gift shop with him to Washington, as well as a copy of the book *Southern Lighthouses*. Sitting in the car with the president, who was about to take off on a flight to some distant locale, Senator Basnight divulged what he knew about the threat to the Cape Hatteras Lighthouse and why it deserved immediate rescue. He was able to convince President Clinton of what it would take to save it and asked that he secure federal funding for the move. Clinton agreed.

The president included $9.8 million to complete the move of the Cape Hatteras light station in his 1999 budget request. Senator Lauch Faircloth had obtained $2 million in 1997 so that the National Park Service could "plan and prepare" for the relocation, but until this point, the additional funding needed had never been allocated.[143] Additionally, the lighthouse was granted National Historic Landmark status on August 8, 1998, further prioritizing its protection. Cheryl wrote in the Outer Banks Lighthouse Society's newsletter about the significance of these events:

> *For the first time in its history, things were falling into place in favor of relocation of the Cape Hatteras Lighthouse. The Park Service committed to the move, public officials favored it, environmentalists advocated it, the lighthouse community applauded it, the budget supported it, and the ocean demanded it.…* [Becoming a National Historic Landmark] *was the same as giving a direct order to the National Park Service that it must protect the lighthouse in any possible way. And since the plans were on the architect's table, money was available, and the high tide line was within 120 feet of the lighthouse's foundation with frequent storms predicted, things began to happen at a rapid pace. In January, 1999, the keepers' quarters and oil house were moved to the new site. The lighthouse was prepped and it, too, would start rolling in June.*[144]

Heavy machinery prepares a "highway in the sand," down which the Cape Hatteras Lighthouse would be rolled, with the help of hydraulic jacks, along a steel track in 1999. *Photo courtesy of the Outer Banks History Center, Mike Booher Collection.*

In January 1999, the principal keeper's quarters, the double keepers' quarters that historically housed the two assistant keepers and their families and the oil house were moved to the new site. The two-hundred-foot tower that kept watch over the island was set to begin its migration in June.

A HEART FOR HERITAGE

It wasn't solely for the sake of science that Cheryl and her group pushed so hard to have the lighthouse moved. The role of history and heritage weighed just as heavily. Many of those opposed to moving the lighthouse cited this reason for wanting it to stay put: their ancestors had kept that light. In fact, many of them had helped build it. Close to one hundred laborers were locally hired and trained and paid a dollar and a half for a day's work.[145] Local families had lived, worked and raised children in the keeper's quarters. To lose the lighthouse would be to lose the collective family history of their small island community, the tangible tie to the memories that Hatteras islanders shared and cherished.

Cheryl knew their stories well. Beginning in the early nineties, she traveled the country researching the keepers and their families responsible for running the nation's lighthouses. She dedicated countless hours to locating descendants and collecting their oral histories, publishing *Lighthouse Families* with Bruce in 1997, which chronicled the bygone way of life in early twentieth-century America.

"I got very interested in interviewing keepers' descendants, it grabbed my heart and I was hooked," she recalls. She found most descendants still living close to the lighthouses where their fathers and grandfathers had been keepers. In a time before GPS or navigation apps, she found her subjects largely by word of mouth. That is, when she could understand the dialect. While driving around a small coastal town in Maine in search of the first descendant she would interview, she got lost and had to stop for directions. A group of fishermen in waders tending their nets at the docks were happy to help, but their brogue was so thick that Cheryl left the encounter as lost as she was before.

After driving around for another hour or so, she finally found the home of the old woman she hoped to interview. It had fallen into disrepair, and she found the elderly descendant of a lighthouse family alone inside. The woman had been widowed for some time but seemed to have forgotten, calling her husband's name throughout the visit. She was able, however, to share stories of a life that revolved around a lighthouse, captivating Cheryl's imagination and curiosity. She went into town and bought groceries, then brought them back to the old woman's house to stock her kitchen. The next day, she contacted the woman's son and told him that he needed to check in on his mother.[146]

Cheryl's big heart led her to connect with dozens of descendants and islanders up and down our nation's coasts and to record their stories. She edited and published *Cape Hatteras Keepers: Oral and Family Histories* in 2001 and *Bodie Island Keepers: Oral and Family Histories* in 2013, cowritten with certified genealogist Sandra MacLean Clunies. Cheryl visited the remote, windswept villages of Hatteras Island, knocking door to door to locate her subjects. In small towns where people tend to be wary of outsiders, she was welcomed into their homes and listened as they told her what life was like in the shadow of a lighthouse. Of the lighthouse families on Hatteras Island, Cheryl wrote:

> *Despite informal schooling and lives with few amenities, they created a proud heritage for their children. A keeper's family was one of the most*

Cheryl Shelton-Roberts and Lee Babb on Portsmouth Island circa 2002. Lee was the last baby born on Portsmouth Island and would return frequently after it was deserted in 1971 to replace flowers in the Babb cemetery. *Photo courtesy of Cheryl-Shelton Roberts.*

> *respected in the community; the job title carried an air of authority. The keeper's wife was often the key coordinator of home and hearth, juggling the responsibilities of raising a large family while attending to all needs that arose around her at the light station. It's worth noting that the children and grandchildren inherited a strong sense of right and wrong, frugality, and dedication to one's job. They also share a strong belief that helping others is an act of human kindness as well as just good common sense.*[147]

Many of the Hatteras islanders who opposed the move in the 1990s shared a family tree with the storied lighthouse families. Their emotional ties to the lighthouse were activating this inherited sense of right and wrong. Their pragmatism and common sense also came into play in so strongly objecting to the lighthouse's relocation. Moving a two-hundred-foot, five-thousand-ton brick tower on an island where resources were already scarce seemed a pipe dream. But it turned out to be possible.

MOVING A LIGHTHOUSE

On July 9, 1999, the Cape Hatteras Lighthouse came to rest upon its new foundation, almost three thousand feet southwest of its original location. After years of debate and uncertainty, the slow, carefully engineered journey took twenty-three days to complete, with a price tag of $11.8 million. The contract to move the lighthouse was awarded to the International Chimney Corporation of Buffalo, New York, which was aided by Expert House Movers of Maryland as well as a handful of other contractors. The National Park Service provides a digestible description of the enormous undertaking involved in moving the lighthouse on its website:

> *In simple terms, the concept of moving the 4,830 ton structure consisted of lifting it off its foundation, transferring the load to a transport system, moving the tower along a prepared move route, and installing it on the new foundation.*
>
> *To accomplish this feat, the original foundation down to the pine timbers was replaced by temporary shoring beams and supports. Then a steel beam mat was inserted over the timber mat with temporary posts on top. As cross beams and main beams were set, the temporary shoring parts and beams were removed. Hydraulic jacks built into the main beams were used to effect the 6 foot raise so that roll beams and rollers could be introduced. After all jacks were shored, using oak cribbing, the system was pressurized and the jacks began lifting. At each lift level, jacks were retracted and shored up in sequence and the system lifted again to 6 feet. At this point it was ready to roll.*

Having been lifted off its foundation and uprooted like a Joe Bell flower from the sand, the lighthouse began its move on June 17, 1999. The support frame that now held its base was rolled along a steel track by roller dollies and push jacks, just five feet at a time. Hydraulic jacks kept the lighthouse aligned, and sixty automated sensors could detect vibration and tilt, within one sixteenth of an inch, as the tower traveled perfectly upright along the tracks. The lighthouse even had its own weather station installed at the top so the crew could monitor wind speed and temperature.

The event spanned three weeks during the Outer Banks' peak tourist season and drew hordes of spectators. Area hotels and campgrounds filled to capacity; local restaurants and businesses thrived. In January, Cheryl and Bruce had published an interpretive booklet called *Moving Hatteras: Relocating the Cape Hatteras Light Station to Safety*. Its aim was to educate the

An aerial view of the Cape Hatteras Lighthouse in 1999, showing the path along which it was moved to its new location, 2,900 feet to the southwest. *Photo by Bruce Roberts, courtesy of Cheryl-Shelton Roberts.*

The Cape Hatteras Lighthouse in its new location, 1,500 feet from the shoreline, 2005. *Photo by Bruce Roberts, courtesy of Cheryl-Shelton Roberts.*

public on the logistics of how the move would work, but it was written in future tense. No one knew if things would go to plan or what would actually happen. Cheryl arrived in Buxton on the second day of the move to behold the spectacle for herself, and she remembers the buzz of excitement moving through the crowd. She noticed copies of *Moving Hatteras* circulating around and saw a friend of hers showing photos from the booklet to a group of captivated onlookers.

"That was a huge healing moment," she recalled. "After all of the blood, sweat and tears it was doing what it was supposed to do."

Without Cheryl's consultation, the meeting with the president may have never happened, the funding may have never come through and the lighthouse may have never been moved. But she kept the faith that if the people truly cared about the lighthouse, as she knew they did, they would allow the facts to prevail one way or another. She credits many hardworking members of the scientific, historical and environmental communities that advocated for the move.

"I think the floating foundation was a surprise to many, I don't think that there were many people that knew about this," she claimed. "There was so much back and forth for years, but in the background, there was a steady push forward because the science supported it. The Lighthouse Society really felt that with awareness, through education, people would care and get involved and support the move. And that is, in the end, what happened. It took about ten years, but it did win out."

With a proud 150-year history, including decades of division over its fate, the Cape Hatteras Lighthouse was preserved for the next century when it was successfully moved to its new location on Hatteras Island. There it stands to this day, approximately 1,500 feet from the ocean, just as it was in 1870. According to the National Park Service, "the decision to relocate the Cape Hatteras Light Station was a sound public policy decision based on the best science and engineering information available." While this summary belies the emotion that colored every aspect of the move, the facts did ultimately guide the decision. Despite intimidation and threats, Cheryl never lost faith that they would win out. Her voice and action in the face of opposition helped save the iconic Cape Hatteras Lighthouse for the generations of people who were guided by its light and for generations to come.

Today, Cheryl remains active with the Outer Banks Lighthouse Society and serves on the board of the U.S. Lighthouse Society, where she is responsible for educational programming and a publication called *Lighthouse Fun for Kids*.

Chapter 7

REMEMBERING THE FREEDMEN'S COLONY

Virginia Tillett, 2000s

If you can cross the creek to Roanoke Island, you will find "safe haven."
—First Light of Freedom marker, Fort Raleigh National Historic Site

It was in February, a time of year when the wet and relentless Outer Banks wind buries itself in your bones, that Union troops landed on Roanoke Island and trekked through the salty, labyrinthine marshes of the Croatan Sound. They outnumbered Confederate forces positioned on the island and easily captured the area in the 1862 battle of Roanoke Island. News of the victory was a beacon in the night. Word spread among the enslaved population of eastern North Carolina that the small Union-occupied island that lay between the mainland and the barrier islands had become a safe haven. Those who reached Roanoke Island reached freedom.

Not Lost but Forgotten: The Roanoke Island Freedmen's Colony

The influx of refugees—labeled "contrabands" by the federal government—led to the creation of the Roanoke Island Freedmen's Colony. This settlement afforded thousands of enslaved people their first taste of freedom since their African ancestors were brought to the shores of Virginia in 1619. It was a settlement as significant and pioneering as Sir Walter Raleigh's legendary "Lost Colony" that had inhabited the same shores almost three hundred

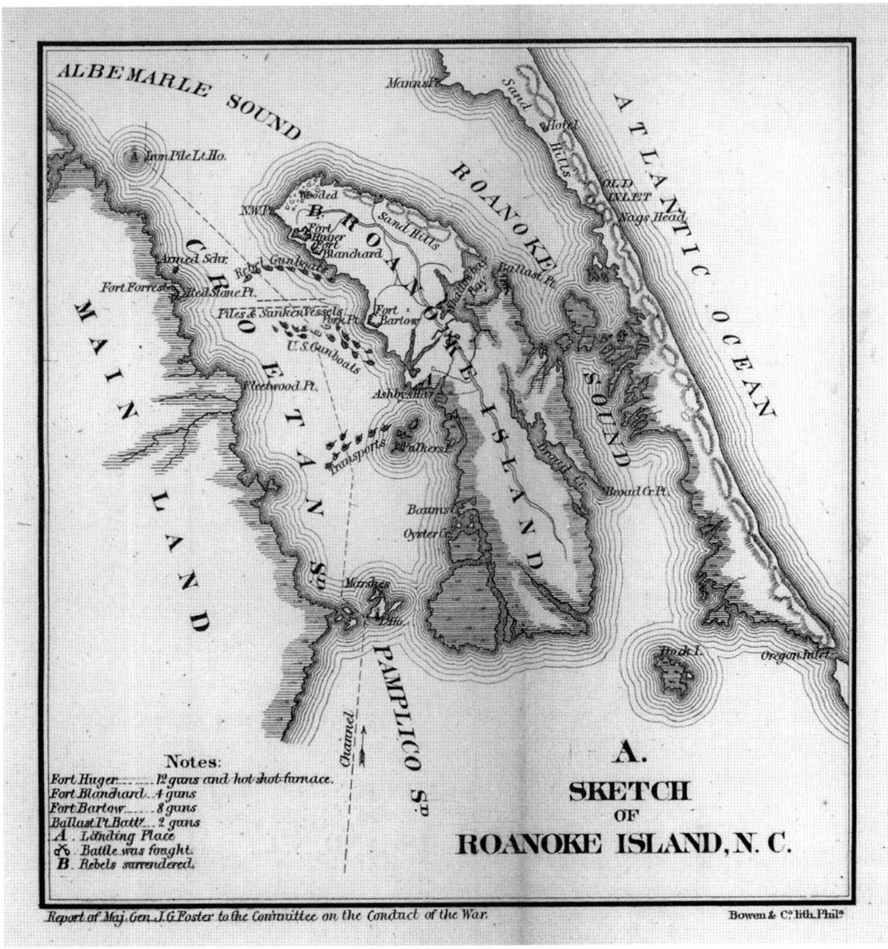

A map of Roanoke Island in 1862, showing the landing site of Union troops. They defeated Confederate forces and began their occupation of the island on February 8, 1862. *Photo courtesy of the Library of Congress, Geography and Map Division.*

years prior. Yet until recently, hardly a soul on Roanoke Island knew anything about it: a colony lost to time and memory, overlooked by the history books.[148]

It wasn't until the new millennium that the general public learned of the Freedmen's Colony, including one of its most noteworthy descendants, Virginia Tillett. In 2001, author and historian Patricia Click published her book *Time Full of Trial: The Roanoke Island Freedmen's Colony, 1862–1867*, and a forgotten chapter of Outer Banks history resurfaced. Fresh out of graduate school, Click became the historian-in-residence for the town of Manteo in 1981 and was tasked with researching the colony of former slaves, to educate the public and broaden the scope of local history leading up to the 400th anniversary of the arrival of English settlers at the Fort Raleigh National Historic Site. Ironically, the arrival of Europeans in North America led to the arrival of slaves; the second colony would not have existed without the first.

Excited by the project, Click dove in, only to find that no physical evidence of the colony's existence on the island remained. Likewise, there was very little memory of it among Roanoke Island's living inhabitants. In the early eighties, residential neighborhoods, tourist attractions and a regional airport had begun to cover much of the North End where the colony was roughly known to have been located, making it difficult to detect any traces of it or map out its borders. Relic hunters over the years, in search of Native American, Civil War and/or Elizabethan artifacts, had removed would-be evidence and disrupted the context of the site in terms of archaeological integrity. In oral history interviews, several elderly African American residents recalled hearing stories of a Black cemetery near Fort Raleigh, of family members who had cooked for Union soldiers and of ancestors who had come to the island during the war. Yet no one was able to offer much that was specific or concrete. The author threw herself into searching through archives, poring over letters, deeds, court documents and other long-forgotten primary sources to piece together the story.[149] Ultimately, the research took twenty years to complete. Once bound, published and distributed, *Time Full of Trial* found its way into the hands of Outer Bankers, and many learned for the first time of their connection to the colony.

A Descendant of the Freedmen: Virginia Simmons Tillett

Born in 1941, Virginia was a decorated Roanoke Island native who committed her life to the service of her community. When she learned of the remarkable history of her fellow African Americans on Roanoke Island and discovered that she was among the descendants of the Freedmen's Colony, she devoted herself to spreading awareness. Of her many accomplishments, memorializing and educating others about the Freedmen's Colony on Roanoke Island became her "biggest thing."[150]

Her forebears—Ashbys, Manns, Simmonses, McCleases and Bryants[151]—were among the resilient women and men who toiled, hoped and persevered in the colony to carve out a future for their families

Virginia Tillett during her time as the continuing education coordinator at the College of the Albemarle. *Photo courtesy of the Outer Banks History Center.*

against all odds. While most of the Freedpeople had come from other parts of northeastern North Carolina, a small number of them were born on Roanoke Island. In 1860, two years before the colony was formed, there were 171 slaves counted among the permanent residents of Roanoke Island, along with twenty-four "free colored" and 395 Whites. After the battle, the formerly enslaved islanders left the farms and homes where they had lived, opting to move into the colony where they were mostly among strangers but free.[152] Though slaves were only enumerated rather than named in census records, there were families with the surname Ashby and Mann on Roanoke Island recorded on the 1860 census, indicating that the branches of Virginia's family with these names were likely those already living in the area prior to the formation of the colony. Her other ancestors may have been among those who fled on foot, crossed bodies of water and risked their lives to reach the "safe haven" of Roanoke Island from other parts of the state.

The first thing the gathering refugees set out to accomplish was to build a house of worship. They built their church from the ample pines on the island and their pulpit from boxes that the Quartermaster's Department had thrown out. Despite having very little to work with, their creativity and resourcefulness served them well. Just weeks after the battle, a second church and the first school for Freedpeople were completed.[153] The refugees recognized the need for religion and education as the foundation for a successful settlement.

Unlike other "contraband camps" in North Carolina (notably Beaufort, Plymouth and New Bern), the Roanoke Island location was the only one ever intended to be a permanent settlement, drawing a parallel to the objectives of Sir Walter's 1587 colony. Similarly, it was the first Freedmen's settlement established in the state and the only one to be officially designated as a "colony." As Click points out, "the colony on Roanoke Island was established with an eye to the future....A camp provided a safe temporary haven for former slaves, while a colony offered the opportunity to mold a permanent community."[154]

A Freedmen's school in South Carolina. The Roanoke Island Freedmen's Colony established several schools between 1862 and 1867. *Photo courtesy of the Library of Congress, William Gladstone Collection.*

THE MANY TRIALS OF THE FREEDMEN'S COLONY

With the goal of permanence in mind, the Roanoke Island Freedmen's Colony was designed as a self-contained, self-sufficient community that turned to fishing, farming and milling lumber for resources and income. In the beginning, as Click points out, "the former slaves were more or less acting on their own" and "claimed shelter wherever they could find it" while "the Union authorities watched the growing population but remained aloof from the day-to-day operation of the camp."[155] However, it soon became apparent that the number of people seeking refuge and freedom on the island would continue to increase. To accommodate and manage the rapid influx of residents, the Reverend Horace James was appointed as the superintendent of Freedmen affairs. He was an abolitionist committed to the fight to end slavery. At the same time, he was an evangelical who didn't believe in social equality among different races. Still, he worked to give the Freedpeople new opportunities and to foster their autonomy in a changing nation.[156]

Many of the Freedmen worked for the army, taking up manual labor jobs—building forts, docks and bridges—that soldiers on the island avoided.

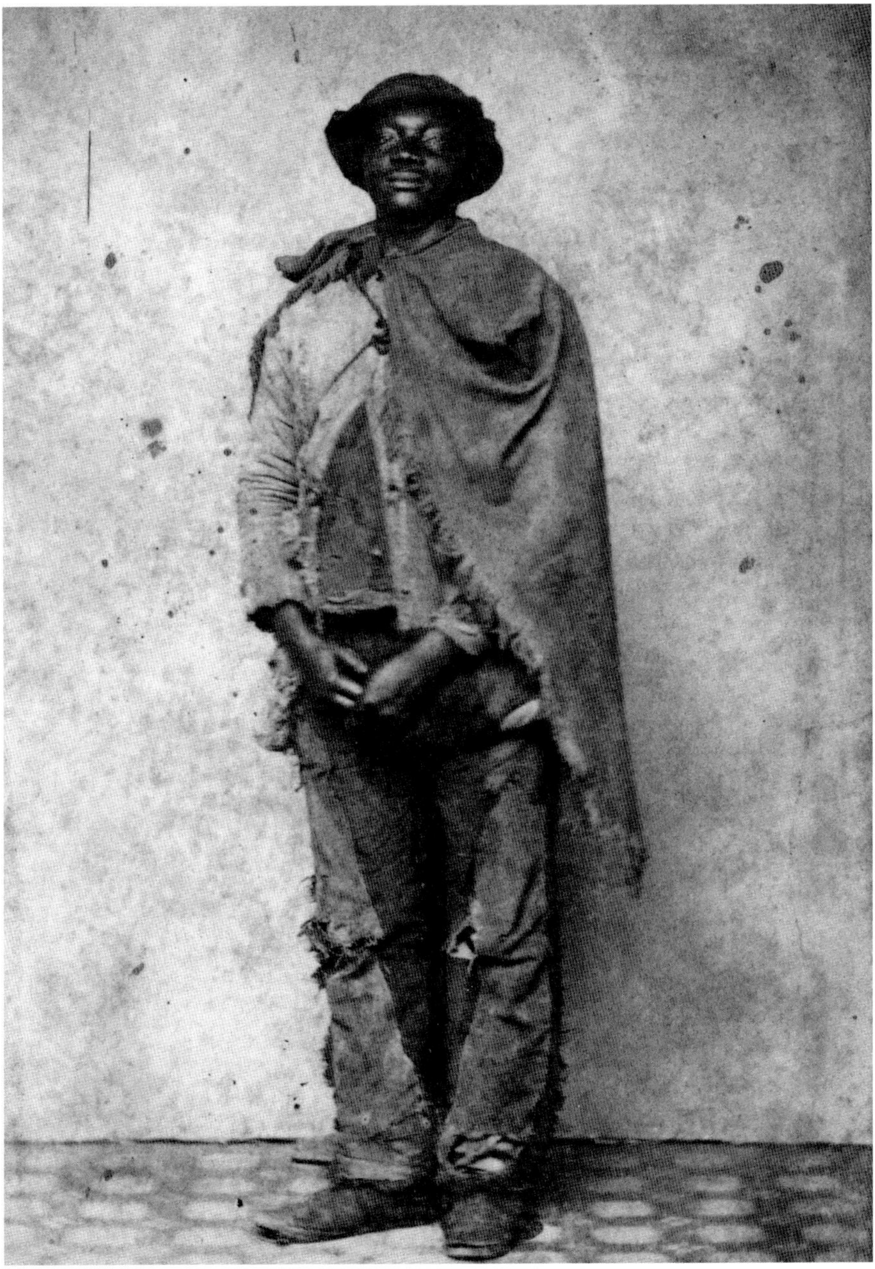

William Headly escaped from a plantation near Raleigh and made it to the Freedmen's colony in New Bern, North Carolina, where he was recognized as free. "Civil War contraband" was written on the back of this photograph. *Photo courtesy of the Library of Congress, William Gladstone Collection.*

An illustration from an 1866 newspaper shows a group of formerly enslaved women sewing at the Freedmen's Union Industrial School in Richmond, Virginia. Freedmen's colonies opened the door to formal education. *Photo courtesy of the Library of Congress.*

Those knowledgeable of the area also served as spies, scouts and guides. Women found employment carrying out domestic work for the soldiers. President Lincoln's Emancipation Proclamation in 1863 allowed Black men to fight for the Union, and many from the colony enlisted. The able-bodied men leaving the island to fight for their families' freedom were told that, in turn, their families would be provided for, with government assistance and rations. The women were left to shoulder the work in the colony and to take care of the children, the elderly and the infirm that remained. Click paints a picture of the shifting demographic:

> *In the absence of their husbands, the women frequently were heads of families that averaged three or four children, although the numbers ranged widely from none to ten or twelve. The women attempted to sustain some semblance of family life, even as they exhausted themselves working for soldiers as cooks, laundresses, or maids. Finding wood to build homes, cutting wood for cooking and heating, and waiting in line for government rations occupied most free hours.*[157]

Yet "the cause of much suffering" came from the withholding of those rations and other broken promises by those in government. While away fighting the war, Freedmen William Benson and Richard Etheridge penned a letter. They claimed:

> *We have served in the U.S. Army faithfully and don [sic] our duty to our Country, for which we thank God that we had the opportunity but at the same time our families are suffering at Roanoke Island, N.C. When we were enlisted in the service we were promised that our wives and families should receive rations from government. The rations for our wives and families have been and are now cut down to one half the regular ration. Consequently three or four days out of every ten days, they have nothing to eat.... Capt. James has not paid the Colored people for their work for near a year and at the same time cuts the ration's off to one half so the people have neither provisions or money to buy it with.*[158]

As it turned out, the assistant superintendent, Holland Streeter, was selling rations intended for those living in the colony to turn a small profit. Benson and Etheridge claimed that Captain James had been notified but chose to look the other way. They also accused White soldiers under Streeter's watch of breaking into homes, robbing gardens, stealing chickens and doing as they pleased, and "if anyone defends their-selves against them they are taken to the guard house for it." Reporting on the colony's progress to his superior, General Foster, it appears that Horace James did complain of the government's failure to pay the Freedmen for their work as promised and pointed out that doing so would help ensure the project's success.[159]

Industry and Infrastructure Bring Improvement to the Colony

Despite hardships, injustices and deteriorating conditions, by 1865 the population of the colony was at its peak, with over three thousand Freedmen living on the otherwise sparsely populated island. New arrivals to the colony lived in the former soldiers' barracks, but conditions quickly grew cramped, and sanitation was exceedingly poor. The Freedpeople did have help in the form of missionaries, mostly White women from New England who came to Roanoke Island to teach in the schools and to help advocate for the colonists. There were several African American teachers among the missionaries, including Martha Culling, a young woman and former slave who started the first Freedmen's school on the island.[160]

Living conditions improved when a grid of avenues and streets was laid out to accommodate the growing community, and over five hundred homes were built in the Freedmen's village over the years. We know that the settlement ran northwest to southeast, roughly from Weir's Point to Pork Point on the island's northwest tip, though there are still no traces of the village's exact location. It was built on "unimproved" and "unoccupied" land confiscated by the Union after naive attempts to purchase it from White landowners.[161] Horace James thought that "there will be no objection on the part of the white inhabitants to selling out."[162] He found himself to be quite mistaken.

Life on an island fosters a deep connection to place and a reliance on community. Roanoke Islanders tended to keep a close circle and were wary of forces outside of it. So after their outright refusal to sell, James noted of the inhabitants that "though not wealthy they are attached to their homes and to the birth and burial places of their fathers." He realized that the wielding of government power to make the sale "compulsory" would be the only way forward.[163]

Lots were drawn and assigned to Freedmen families to clear and build their homes upon. In true Outer Banks fashion, they used whatever materials they

A group of women and girls outside of a Freedmen's school in South Carolina, taken by army photographer Samuel Cooley. *Photo courtesy of the Library of Congress, William Gladstone Collection.*

were able to find or salvage on the island. The houses were mostly built from pine and cypress and featured chimneys made from sticks and mud. The one-room homes were drafty and rudimentary, but "the most significant characteristic of the houses was that they belonged to their builders, who were apparently elated by that prospect." Horace James observed that "they are so animated by the prospect of a homestead of their own…that they labor, every spare moment by night as well as by day."[164]

In addition to owning homes, the colonists were able to marry, preach, gather for worship, be paid for their work and learn to read and write for the first time in their lives. They were devoted to keeping their families together, preserving their culture and fostering a sense of community while navigating and cherishing their newfound freedom.

Breaking Down Barriers: Virginia Tillett's Life of Service

A century later, Virginia's life would also be marked by notable "firsts." For twenty years she served on the Dare County Board of Education and was the first woman and first person of color to serve in the positions of chairman and vice chairman of the board. In 2002, she was elected to the Dare County Board of Commissioners, on which she served for twelve years before being appointed to the Dare County Board of Elections in 2018 and serving until 2020.[165] With innumerable projects and improvements to her name, she was beloved by the Outer Banks for her boundless compassion for the community and her unshakeable ambition.

Like many Outer Bankers, Virginia got her start in the service industry, working at restaurants, hotels and motels that catered to the area's seasonal tourists. "Then I got lucky," she said,[166] when she got a job as the cook at Dare County's Head Start center, a federally funded childcare program focused on supporting low-income families. Here she was able to nurture children with healthy meals and, later, to feed their growing minds. She became a teacher's aide and continued her own education, until she was a head teacher by the time she left Head Start in 1974. She went on to work for the Dare County Library and became known fondly as the "bookmobile lady" for driving the county's mobile library down to Hatteras Island to serve isolated residents who would otherwise have to make visiting the library an all-day affair. She next lent her talents to the College of the Albemarle as an assistant dean and as the coordinator

Dare County Library staff in 1976. Virginia Tillett, seated in the front row, is remembered fondly by many Dare County residents for driving the bookmobile. *Photo courtesy of the Outer Banks History Center.*

of continuing education for the Workforce Development program. Here she spearheaded the launch of the nursing aid, engine repair, welding and boatbuilding programs, opening up regionally specific career paths to area residents.[167]

Virginia Tillett is sworn into office for the Dare County Board of Elections in 2018. *Photo courtesy of the Dare County Board of Elections.*

Born and raised on Roanoke Island by Earlene and Seward Simmons, Virginia was guided by the same tenets of perseverance and resilience that her ancestors in the Freedmen's Colony would have relied on, ideals passed down through generations, even while stories of life in the colony were lost.

"It was born in my blood to always keep your head up high, to know what you're talking about when you speak, and to be nice to everyone," Virginia proclaimed in a 2019 interview, adding how important it is to "believe in the Lord, Jesus Christ and get that education!" She has fond memories of her girlhood on the island with her deeply rooted family, including her great-grandmother Alice Ashby and grandmother Lila Ashby, who was known for her handcrafts and who kept a "tourist house," or bed-and-breakfast. Lila was known as "one of the best businesswomen on Roanoke Island."[168] Virginia married William "Snooks" Tillett, also a descendant of the Freedmen, and raised two sons among the tight-knit community of Roanoke Island.

At a 2019 service at the Fort Raleigh National Historic Site marking the 400th anniversary of African slaves' arrival on our shores, Virginia remarked that "just about every black person here is related to someone who is a descendant of the Freedmen's Colony."[169] Yet despite this significant historical tie, "the African American experience on Roanoke Island is perpetually minimized or absent from most historical accounts of the area," in the words of one paper.[170] That our collective history remembers and glorifies an attempted settlement from the 1500s and virtually forgot one from the late 1800s is a testament to this claim. The fact that "African Americans on the Outer Banks and on Roanoke Island did not experience large-scale desegregation until the National Civil Rights Act was passed in 1964"[171] adds weight to Virginia's accomplishments. Just several years after desegregation, she ran for and secured a spot on the school board of a predominantly White community, helping to shape policy in the changing landscape of public schools. She spent twenty years on the Board of Education, followed by another twelve as a county commissioner. Throughout her thirty-two-year career as an elected official, she was a constant champion of education and an advocate for diversity and inclusion.

For her long-standing service to the community, Virginia was awarded the Order of the Long Leaf Pine by the governor of North Carolina, as well as the Citizen of the Year Award by the Dare County Chamber of Commerce in 2006. In 2015, she was named the Dare County Outstanding Citizen of the Year, and in 2021 she accepted the North Carolina Black Alliance Trailblazer Award for her "dedication to community and servant leadership over the years."

COMMEMORATING THE FORGOTTEN FREEDMEN

Once retired, Virginia remained active with Haven Creek Baptist Church, established by the Freedmen during the Civil War,[172] and served as president of the Roanoke Island Freedmen's Colony Preservation Association. She used her voice and her platform as a cherished member of the community to bring these forgotten pages of history to the public. Each year she joined forces with her neighbors and fellow descendants Arvilla Bowser and Delerva Collins to coordinate a festival and blues jam to celebrate and remember the contributions of the Freedmen's Colony.[173]

Though no physical traces of the colony remain on the island, the Fort Raleigh National Historic Site is now home to the First Light of Freedom marker, an understated yet stoic monument to its memory. It stands in the bricked plaza of the Visitor's Center, where the branches of encircling oaks seem to bow down in reverence. Thanks to the collaboration of Virginia, Arvilla and Delerva with the Dare County Heritage Trail committee, the marker was erected and dedicated in 2001, the same year that Click's *Time*

Full of Trial reached the shelves. The site became designated as part of the National Underground Railroad Network to Freedom. Made of polished black granite, the marker depicts an enslaved family rejoicing at the site of the sun parting the clouds over a distant hill. Elevating a proud history of firsts on the Outer Banks, it reminds viewers of the other lost colony that carved out a life on the same hallowed ground. It reads: "Once again, this small island, site of the first attempt at permanent settlement in the New World, became a land of historic beginnings."

With every beginning there comes an end. While questions still loom over the Lost Colony's end, the end of the Freedmen's Colony is well documented. In 1865, President Andrew Johnson issued an amnesty proclamation returning the land inhabited by the Freedmen to its former owners, provided that they could show proof of ownership and requiring them to swear an oath of allegiance to the United States government. The president did not indicate, in policy or in practice, much concern over reparations for former slaves.[174] What started as a group of people flocking to the Union-occupied island for a chance at freedom evolved, with government support and backing, into an attempted permanent settlement. Ultimately, several unfortunate factors kept the colony from flourishing like it might have and led the government's interest and support to dwindle and the settlement to come to an end. As Click sums up:

> *The light industries and domestic manufacturing that were supposed to make the colony self-sufficient had never materialized. A succession of poor shad seasons yielded less than had been invested in nets, and hopes for scuppernong wine production were never met. Without jobs or some alternate support, the colonists could not afford to rent lands or maintain themselves on the island, and conditions in the colony rapidly deteriorated for freed people. Even though Horace James complained about returning land to former slave owners, he realized that land restoration was now the only thing that could compel the colonists to return to the mainland and find jobs to support themselves.*[175]

The government's goal of aiding in the establishment of a self-sufficient community of freed slaves shifted to an attempt to discourage them from remaining there and drive them back to the mainland, where they might find more opportunities. To achieve this, the "Freedmen's Bureau officials encouraged resettlement by making life on the island difficult for the colonists," mainly through cutting rations, restoring land to former owners

The First Light of Freedom marker at the Fort Raleigh National Historic Site commemorates the Roanoke Island Freedmen's Colony. No physical evidence of the colony that once existed on the island's north end remains. *Photo courtesy of Lauren Cowart.*

(who often would not allow Freedpeople to rent or purchase lots in order to stay) and even transporting people back to the mainland themselves.[176]

The population of the colony was reduced to only 950 by the start of 1867, which saw a harsh and inhospitable winter. Heavy storms assaulted the barrier islands, and boats weren't able to bring needed supplies when the sound froze over. By this time, there were fewer than 20 people receiving government rations, leaving the vast majority to face a dire lack of resources.[177]

One northern missionary, still attempting to operate schools in the failing colony, remarked that "the best of the people have left the island, the lazy and wicked ones remain....They are *desperate*."[178] But most of those who remained were Roanoke Island natives. Far from idle and helpless, they were survivors, loyal to their birthplace. With little experience in agriculture or plantation labor, leaving the land where they had been born and raised for farms farther inland offered them few prospects. On the island, they had learned to fish the waters, hunt fowl and forage in the woods. They knew the land and the paths through the marsh like the lines in their palms. It was the birth and burial place of their fathers. They petitioned to be allowed to stay so that they might eventually "lay their bones to mingle with the dust of their childhood's home."[179]

The Roanoke Island Freedmen's Colony was disbanded in 1867, and the remaining residents faced an uncertain future. They were forced to leave the land where they had been allowed (and initially encouraged) by the government to settle. The land was returned to its previous owners, and though the colonists had been told by the Freedmen's Bureau that they would be able to dismantle their homes and carry the building materials with them when they relocated, these owners prevented them from doing so.[180] It is said that the structures were all burned or otherwise destroyed.[181]

RETAINING ROANOKE ISLAND ROOTS

Despite abandonment and hardship, a few hundred members of the former colony could not be daunted and chose to remain on Roanoke Island. Most were those who had been born and raised on the island, but some were those who had fled there during the war. In 1868, eleven families came together to purchase two hundred acres on the west side of Roanoke Island from the heirs of Thomas A. Dough, which became known as the "California Tract." At least three other Freedmen owned parcels of land on the island as well.[182]

The former slaves turned landowners banded together, along with those who were living as "free colored" people prior to the war, to establish a close-knit Black community of roughly three hundred people on Roanoke Island by 1870, according to that year's census. Now was their time to rise up from the ashes. By attaining land, they were able to put down roots and had a chance at building wealth. Many were now self-employed, rather than working in White households or for White employers. They were able to carve out lives for themselves that might offer stability and opportunity for generations to come.

Acknowledging the foundation laid by her ancestors, Virginia knew that "having been raised here on Roanoke Island, it afforded me opportunities. In other small towns like Manteo, people would not have had the opportunities that I've had. I've been blessed."[183] Author Patricia Click agrees, noting in her book that "tradition on the island holds that segregation was never as strict there as it was in other parts of northeastern North Carolina; Blacks and Whites struggled alike and sometimes even together to make ends meet."[184]

In her later years, Virginia enjoyed talking with schools and community groups to raise awareness of the Freedmen's Colony, pushing to have it incorporated into North Carolina's history curriculum. She observed that "adults sometimes don't know what to ask because they don't know whether they are going to offend." She explained that she was often able to reach the adults with the disclaimer that "what happened 200 years ago, neither one of us had any control over. We accept what happened and move on. But it's a part of history, so we're going to talk about it in a positive light."[185]

Virginia's accepting and forgiving approach often inspired people to dig up and share old family heirlooms, photos, letters or documents in hopes that they might help her or other Black families on Roanoke Island patch in the missing pieces of their family histories. When it came to the young people she spoke to about the Freedmen's Colony, her belief was this:

> *The history needs to be told. Our young folks need to be reminded. Because if you do not know where you came from, you certainly don't know where you're going…I would like to see young folks embrace their history and how important it is. I look at young folks now that will say to me, "I'm not going to vote." But I'm saying, your ancestors died so you could vote….If I had a mission, it would be to help them understand where they came from and how to move forward….I want them to know how hard their ancestors worked, fought and died for them to have a better life. That's what I want them to know.*[186]

Many descendants of the Freedmen's Colony still call Manteo's California neighborhood home today. They are Virginia's family, her neighbors and friends. Their history is her history, and sharing it became her lasting legacy. Virginia Simmons Tillett passed away on October 7, 2021, but her impact on countless aspects of life on the Outer Banks lives on. Anyone who has sent a child to school, checked out a book, continued their education or voted in Dare County in the past sixty years has Virginia to thank for making it a better and more inclusive experience. She lived for the people: those in her life and those who came before her. She gave a voice to all those that were silenced in the sweep of time, uncovering their path to freedom on Roanoke Island, the land of new beginnings.

NOTES

Chapter 1

1. Michael Leroy Oberg, *The Head in Edward Nugent's Hand: Roanoke's Forgotten Indians* (Philadelphia: University of Pennsylvania Press, 2008), 3.
2. Ibid., 4.
3. Ibid., 8.
4. David Beers Quinn, *The Roanoke Voyages 1584–1590: Documents to Illustrate the English Voyages to North America under the Patent Granted to Walter Raleigh in 1584*, vols. 1–2 (Farnham, UK, and Burlington, VT: Ashgate, for the Hakluyt Society, 1952; digitized 2010), 518.
5. Ibid., 523.
6. Ibid.
7. Oberg, *Head in Edward Nugent's Hand*, 113.
8. Ibid., 94.
9. Ibid., 98.
10. Ibid., 96–98.
11. Ibid., xii–xiv.
12. Ibid., 98–100.
13. Ibid., 107–8.
14. Ibid., 114.
15. Ibid., 115.
16. Quinn, *Roanoke Voyages*, 526.
17. Oberg, *Head in Edward Nugent's Hand*, 527.
18. Quinn, *Roanoke Voyages*, 530.

19. Ibid.
20. Oberg, *Head in Edward Nugent's Hand*, 123.
21. "John White's Attempt to Rescue the Roanoke Colonists," National Humanities Center, accessed June 1, 2021, http://nationalhumanitiescenter.org/pds/amerbegin/exploration/text6/white.pdf.
22. Oberg, *Head in Edward Nugent's Hand*, 125–26.
23. Ibid., 127–31.
24. Ibid., 139; T. Mike Childs and Kelly Agan, "The Dare Stones," NCPedia, 2013 and 2019, https://www.ncpedia.org/dare-stones.
25. "The Dare Stones," Brenau University, accessed May 1, 2021, https://www.brenau.edu/darestones/. I have chosen to modify the old English spellings into modern American English where possible, for the ease of the reader.
26. Oberg, *Head in Edward Nugent's Hand*, 142.

Chapter 2

27. "Was 105 Years Old," *Wilmington Morning Star*, March 12, 1914.
28. Lu Ann Jones and Amy Glass, *Everyone Helped His Neighbor: Memories of Nags Head Woods* (Chapel Hill: University of North Carolina Press, 2018), 13.
29. H.R. McIlwaine, ed., *Minutes of the Council and General Court of Colonial Virginia: 1622–1632, 1670–1676 with Notes and Excerpts from Original Counsel and General Court Records into 1683, Now Lost* (Richmond: Virginia State Library, 1924), 437.
30. Paul Heinegg, *Free African Americans of North Carolina and Virginia* (Baltimore: Genealogical Publishing, 2020), http://www.freeafricanamericans.com/Virginia_NC.htm.
31. "Roanoke-Hatteras Tribal History," Algonquian Indians of North Carolina, Inc., accessed November 1, 2021, http://www.ncalgonquians.com/tribalhistory.html. There was a community of Native American descendants on Roanoke Island known as "Bowser Town." The Benjamin Bowser branch of the Bowser family was free in 1860 and had known Indigenous ancestry. Before moving to Roanoke Island, they lived in Powell's Point, on Colington Island and in parts of the Dare County mainland. It is possible that Chrissy Bowser could have been free and living somewhere other than Roanoke Island prior to 1870, providing another explanation of her absence from antebellum census records aside from enslavement.

32. United States Federal Census, Population Schedule for Currituck County, NC, 1860. With the exception of a William and Elizabeth Bowser who lived together in the home of Lovey Etheridge.
33. Penne Smith, *Etheridge Homeplace: A History* (Manteo: Outer Banks Conservationists, 2001), 36.
34. Roanoke Island was part of Currituck County prior to the creation of Dare County in 1870.
35. United States Federal Census, Population Schedule for Dare County, Nags Head Township NC, 1870 and 1880.
36. Annika Neklason, "The Mystery Behind Frederick Douglass's Birthday," *Atlantic*, February 17, 2018, https://www.theatlantic.com/national/archive/2018/02/the-mystery-behind-frederick-douglasss-birthday/553571/.
37. Corinne Saunders, "Roanoke-Hatteras Algonquian: The Tribe That Never Left," *Coastal Review*, October 11, 2021, https://coastalreview.org/2021/10/roanoke-hatteras-algonquian-the-tribe-that-never-left/.
38. Marilyn Berry Morrison, chief of the Roanoke-Hatteras tribe of the Algonquian Indians of North Carolina, in conversation with the author, November 12, 2021.
39. 1870 Federal Census.
40. Smith, *Etheridge Homeplace*, 37.
41. Arvilla Tillett Bowser and Lindsey Bowser, *Roanoke Island: The Forgotten Colony* (Chesapeake: Maximilian Press Publishers, 2002), 61.
42. 1870 Federal Census. An eighty-year-old Black male named Thomas Hill with the same birth date appears on the 1900 census, suggesting that he may have come back to Roanoke Island in his later years.
43. Smith, *Etheridge Homeplace*, 36.
44. George Baum et al. to Colonel Charles Benzoni, "The Undersigned Colored Citizens of Roanoke Island, December 23, 1867," Freedmen's Bureau Assistant Commissioner Records, 1862–1870. https://www.roanokefreedmenscolony.com/freedmn3.pdf.
45. Patricia Click, *Time Full of Trial: The Roanoke Island Freedmen's Colony, 1862–1867* (Chapel Hill: University of North Carolina Press, 2001), 268.
46. Ibid., 198.
47. Smith, *Etheridge Homeplace*, 17.
48. Ibid., 31. John B. Etheridge, who was White, was most likely the father of Richard Etheridge. Richard grew up as a slave in the household of John B. Etheridge but did learn to read and write.
49. Ibid., 19–20.

50. Ibid., 37.
51. David Wright and David Zoby, *Fire on the Beach: Recovering the Lost Story of Richard Etheridge and the Pea Island Lifesavers* (New York: Simon & Schuster, 2000), 45.
52. Smith, *Etheridge Homeplace*, 37.
53. "Was 105 Years Old," 1914.
54. Ibid.
55. Smith, *Etheridge Homeplace*, 38.
56. Ibid., 37–38.

Chapter 3

57. William J. Tate, "With the Wrights at Kitty Hawk: Anniversary of First Flight Twenty-Five Years Ago," in *The Published Writings of Wilbur and Orville Wright*, ed. Peter L. Jakab and Rick Young (Washington: Smithsonian Books, 2000), 280.
58. Thomas C. Parramore, *First to Fly: North Carolina and the Beginnings of Aviation* (Chapel Hill: University of North Carolina Press, 2002), 292.
59. Glen Duffy, "On a Windy March Night, Remembering the Wright Brothers," *Atlantic City Press*, March 23, 1980.
60. William J. Tate, "General Correspondence 1900–1909," Wilbur Wright and Orville Wright papers, 1809–1979, Library of Congress, manuscript/mixed material, accessed January 11, 2020, from https://www.loc.gov/item/wright002562/.
61. Tate, "With the Wrights at Kitty Hawk," 280.
62. Ibid., 281.
63. David McCullough, *The Wright Brothers* (New York: Simon and Schuster, 2015), 46.
64. Edward Hitzel, "The Eye Witness: Kitty Hawk to the Space Shuttle," *Atlantic City Press*, May 3, 1981.
65. Tate, "With the Wrights at Kitty Hawk," 281.
66. Ibid., 279.
67. Ibid., 280.
68. McCullough, *Wright Brothers*, 47.
69. Ibid., 47, 56.
70. Charlotte Johnson, "Kitty Hawk History: The Wright Brothers and a Little Girl," *Atlantic City Press*, November 27, 1934.
71. Mark E. Heisler, "Area Woman's Father Immortalized Kitty Hawk," *Atlantic City Press*, April 23, 1961.

72. Parramore, *First to Fly*, 288.
73. Ibid., 290.
74. Ibid.
75. Hitzel, "Eye Witness." Irene's grandmother was likely Sophia Toler, though I could not confirm.
76. Parramore, *First to Fly*, 293.
77. Ibid., 290.
78. Raymond Harbison, "Brigantine Woman Saw Wright Brothers Flight," *Atlantic City Press*, December 17, 1956.
79. Heisler, "Area Woman's Father."
80. Parramore, *First to Fly*, 292.
81. History.com editors, "Amelia Earhart," *History.com*, March 16, 2021, https://www.history.com/topics/exploration/amelia-earhart.
82. Louis Marden, "She Wore the World's First Wings," *Outer Banks Magazine*, 1984.
83. Johnson, "Kitty Hawk History."
84. Harbison, "Brigantine Woman."
85. Tammi Pittaro, granddaughter of Irene Tate Severn, in conversation with the author March 13, 2021.
86. Hitzel, "Eye Witness."

Chapter 4

87. Jones and Glass, *Everyone Helped His Neighbor*, 13.
88. The Nature Conservancy, "Nags Head Woods Preserve," *The Nature Conservancy*, 2021, https://www.nature.org/en-us/get-involved/how-to-help/places-we-protect/nags-head-woods-ecological-preserve/.
89. Radford Tillett, "Radford and Margie Tillett Interview—Life in Nags Head Woods—Everyone Helped His Neighbor," interview by the Town of Kill Devil Hills, April 1, 2020, YouTube video, https://youtu.be/oEge0jIO5iA.
90. Jones and Glass, *Everyone Helped His Neighbor*, back cover.
91. Dorothy Hope and Chaz Winkler, "National Register Registration Form Amendment for Mattie Midgett's Store and House, Nags Head NC" (Nags Head: Outer Banks Beachcomber Museum, 2019), 1. This three hundred–acre portion of their property was purchased in 1916 from fellow Lifesaving Service surfman Robert L. Wescott, after the Wrights had completed the first flight.

92. Edward R. Outlaw Jr., *Old Nag's Head* (Norfolk: Liskey Lithograph, 1956), 28.
93. Jones and Glass, *Everyone Helped His Neighbor*, 46.
94. Penne Robbins, "Beachcomber: The Lady of the Sand," *The Virginia Pilot Online*, 2006, https://www.pilotonline.com/entertainment/article_dd2741c4-00cf-5a4b-87d5-b2679a39a636.html.
95. Jones and Glass, *Everyone Helped His Neighbor*, 38.
96. Lorraine Eaton, "The Collector," *Outer Banks Magazine*, 1996, reprinted with permission by C&D, 2006, p. 2, https://www.presnc.org/files/2019/07/Nellie_Booklet_cover-photo-4008-South-Virginia-Dare.pdf.
97. Robbins, "Beachcomber."
98. Jones and Glass, *Everyone Helped His Neighbor,* 47.
99. Eaton, "The Collector," 3.
100. Hope and Winkler, "National Register," 2.
101. Eaton, "The Collector," 3.
102. Ibid., 5.
103. Dorothy Hope and Chaz Winkler in discussion with the author, March 2020.
104. Ibid.
105. Eaton, "The Collector," 6.
106. Ibid., 7.
107. Outer Banks Visitors Bureau, *Visitation Figures at Key Sites 2016–2020* (Manteo: Outer Banks Visitors Bureau, 2021).
108. Eaton, "The Collector," 8.
109. Dorothy Hope and Chaz Winkler in discussion with the author, March 2020.

Chapter 5

110. "Jockey's Ridge: Public-Private Interests Reconciled at the Nation's Most Lofty Sand Pile," *We the People of North Carolina,* June 1975.
111. John Alexander and James Lazell, *Ribbon of Sand: The Amazing Convergence of the Ocean and the Outer Banks* (Chapel Hill: University of North Carolina Press, 2000), 49.
112. Sarah Perry, "Where Sand Meets Sky: Jockey's Ridge," *Our State*, January 1, 2013, https://www.ourstate.com/jockeys-ridge/.
113. "Jockey's Ridge: Public-Private Interests Reconciled."
114. Ibid.

115. Perry, "Where Sand Meets Sky."
116. Ann-Cabell Baum in discussion with the author, July 2021.
117. Sarah Downing, *Vintage Outer Banks: Shifting Sands and Bygone Beaches* (Charleston: The History Press, 2008), chap. 11.
118. Chris Kidder, "At Nags Head, Tide Is Turning in Favor of the Local History," *Greensboro News & Record*, April 7, 1990, updated January 25, 2015, https://greensboro.com/at-nags-head-tide-is-turning-in-favor-of-the-local-history/article_f4ce19d4-a4a9-5b51-82a8-5bde13251922.html; Ann-Cabell Baum in discussion with the author, July 2021.
119. Ann-Cabell Baum in discussion with the author, July 2021.
120. Arthur W. Cooper, *My Years in Public Service: An Ecologist's Venture into Government* (Bloomington: AuthorHouse, 2017), chap. 8.
121. Ibid.; "Jockey's Ridge: Public-Private Interests Reconciled."
122. *Jockey's Ridge for All the People*, directed by Ronald Hagell (Chapel Hill, NC: CPT Film Laboratory, 1976). Courtesy of the State Archives of North Carolina.
123. "Association Seeks to Preserve Chicamacomico Lifesaving Station," *Statesville Record & Landmark*, August 4, 1977, https://www.newspapers.com/newspage/4004099/
124. Downing, *Vintage Outer Banks*, chap. 11.
125. Mark Murrell, "Local Group Backs Raising Sunken Warship," *Daily Tarheel*, December 1, 1978.
126. Perry, "Where Sand Meets Sky."

Chapter 6

127. "Cape Hatteras Light Station," National Park Service, accessed August 1, 2021, https://www.nps.gov/caha/planyourvisit/chls.htm.
128. "John White's Attempt to Rescue the Roanoke Colonists," National Humanities Center, accessed June 1, 2021, http://nationalhumanitiescenter.org/pds/amerbegin/exploration/text6/white.pdf.
129. "Cape Hatteras Light Station."
130. "Managed Retreat," *99% Invisible* podcast, episode 293, January 30, 2018, accessed January 1, 2021, https://99percentinvisible.org/episode/managed-retreat/.
131. "Cape Hatteras Light Station."
132. Ibid.
133. "Managed Retreat."

134. Cheryl-Shelton Roberts in discussion with the author, August 2021.
135. Ibid.
136. "Cape Hatteras Light Station"; "Managed Retreat."
137. "Faircloth, Jones Announce Final Schedule for Public Meeting on Saving the Lighthouse," *Coastland Times*, April 5, 1998.
138. Ibid.
139. "Lighthouse Preservation Proponents Facts Presentation April 7, Raleigh," *Coastland Times*, April 5, 1998.
140. Cheryl Shelton-Roberts in discussion with the author, August 2021.
141. Dave Schulty, "Lighthouse Fate Pondered After Emotional Meeting," *Coastland Times*, April 12, 1998.
142. Ibid.
143. Cheryl Shelton-Roberts, "Senate Resolution 507 Declared August 7, 2013, National Lighthouse & Lighthouse Preservation Day," Outer Banks Lighthouse Society, https://www.outerbankslighthousesociety.org/national_lighthouse_day.html.
144. Ibid.
145. "Cape Hatteras Light Station."
146. Cheryl-Shelton Roberts in discussion with the author, August 2021.
147. Cheryl-Shelton Roberts, "A Keeper's Life," *Our State*, May 2001.

Chapter 7

148. Patricia Click, *Time Full of Trial: The Roanoke Island Freedmen's Colony, 1862–1867* (Chapel Hill: University of North Carolina Press, 2001), 200.
149. Ibid., preface, 200–201.
150. "Virginia Tillett: A Dare County Trailblazer," Current TV, Manteo, NC, 2021, YouTube video, https://youtu.be/Y5jCQu9DyNo.
151. Ibid.
152. Click, *Time Full of Trial*, 196.
153. Ibid., 35.
154. Ibid., 12.
155. Ibid., 36.
156. Ibid., 14.
157. Ibid., 91.
158. Sergeant Richard Etheridge and William Benson to General Howard, May or June 1865, Office of the Assistant Commissioner of North

Carolina, Letters Received, Record Group 105, Series 2453, Microfilm 843, Reel 16, National Archives.

159. Click, *Time Full of Trial*, 52–53.

160. Ibid., 85.

161. Ibid., 46–48.

162. Patricia C. Click, "How Andrew Johnson Doomed the Roanoke Island Freedmen's Colony," *Slate*, November 8, 2017, https://slate.com/human-interest/2017/11/how-president-johnson-doomed-efforts-to-secure-land-for-former-slaves.html.

163. Ibid.

164. Click, *Time Full of Trial*, 51–52.

165. Mary Helen Goodloe-Murphy, "Community Mourns Death of Virginia Simmons Tillett," *Coastland Times*, October 11, 2021, https://www.thecoastlandtimes.com/2021/10/11/community-mourns-death-of-virginia-simmons-tillett/.

166. "Virginia Tillett: A Dare County Trailblazer," Current TV.

167. Ibid.

168. "Celebrating Black History Month on the Outer Banks—The Freedmen's Colony," Roanoke Island Festival Park, Manteo, NC, 2019, YouTube video, https://youtu.be/sRB9815_LYw.

169. Catherine Kozak, "Remembrance Marks African Slaves' Arrival," *CoastalReview.org*, August 30, 2019, https://coastalreview.org/2019/08/remembrance-marks-african-slaves-arrival/.

170. Jeannine Lynn Carpenter, "The Lost Community of the Outer Banks: African American Speech on Roanoke Island" (master's thesis, North Carolina State University, 2004), 28, https://repository.lib.ncsu.edu/bitstream/handle/1840.16/2338/etd.pdf.

171. Ibid.

172. Aaron Tuell, "First in Freedom: A Culture of Diversity on the Outer Banks," OuterBanks.org, June 18, 2021, https://www.outerbanks.org/blog/post/first-in-freedom-a-culture-of-diversity-on-the-outer-banks/.

173. Kathleen Angione, "The Freedmen of Roanoke Island: The Other Lost Colony," *Coastwatch*, 2005, https://ncseagrant.ncsu.edu/coastwatch/previous-issues/2005-2/holiday-2005/the-freedmen-of-roanoke-island-the-other-lost-colony/.

174. Click, "How Andrew Johnson Doomed the Roanoke Island Freedmen's Colony."

175. Ibid.

176. Click, *Time Full of Trial*, 178, 187.

177. Ibid., 188.
178. Ibid.
179. Ibid., 188, 266.
180. Ibid., 197.
181. Michael Zatarga (National Park Service, Fort Raleigh National Historic Site) in discussion with the author, August 2021.
182. Click, *Time Full of Trial*, 196–97.
183. "Virginia Tillett: A Dare County Trailblazer," Current TV.
184. Click, *Time Full of Trial*, 205.
185. Angione, "The Freedmen of Roanoke Island."
186. Outer Banks Forever (@obxparksforever), "We are incredibly saddened to hear that Ms. Virginia Tillett, a Dare County educator and community leader, has passed away," Instagram photo caption, October 8, 2021, https://www.instagram.com/p/CUxq1AfBmEY/?utm_medium=copy_link.

INDEX

J

K

L

M

N

O

P

Q

R

ABOUT THE AUTHOR

Hannah Bunn West has a degree in creative nonfiction from the University of North Carolina at Wilmington, as well as a teaching certificate from UNCW's Watson School of Education. She has taught at the elementary and high school level and is a mother of two. Born and raised on the Outer Banks of North Carolina, she is a freelance writer passionate about sharing the area's beauty and rich history with others. She writes about the stories, successes and human experiences of the people who inhabit these barrier islands, with the hope to advocate and inspire. This is her first book.

Visit us at
www.historypress.com